Peddling Protectionism

Peddling Protectionism

Smoot-Hawley and
the Great Depression

Douglas A. Irwin

Princeton University Press
Princeton and Oxford

Published by Princeton University Press, 41 William Street,
Princeton, New Jersey 08540
In the United Kingdom: Princeton University Press, 6 Oxford Street,
Woodstock, Oxfordshire OX20 1TW
press.princeton.edu

Excerpts from "Invocation" by Ogden Nash, copyright © 1930 by
Ogden Nash, reprinted by permission of Curtis Brown, Ltd.

Library of Congress Cataloging-in-Publication Data
Irwin, Douglas A., 1962–
Peddling protectionism : Smoot-Hawley and the Great Depression /
Douglas A. Irwin.
p.   cm.
Includes bibliographical references and index.
ISBN 978-0-691-15032-1 (hardcover : alk. paper)   1. Tariff—
United States—History—20th century.   2. United States—Com-
mercial policy—History—20th century.   3. United States—Eco-
nomic conditions—20th century.   4. Protectionism—United
States.   5. Depressions—1929—United States.   6. United States.
Tariff Act of 1930.   I. Title.
HF1756.I685 2011
382'.7097309043—dc22   2010041081

British Library Cataloging-in-Publication Data is available
This book has been composed in Janson Text LT Std
Designed by Marcella Engel Roberts

Printed on acid-free paper. ∞

Printed in the United States of America

1 3 5 7 9 10 8 6 4 2

Contents

Peddling Protectionism

Introduction

On November 9, 1993, Vice President Al Gore and Texas billionaire and former presidential candidate Ross Perot debated the controversial North American Free Trade Agreement (NAFTA) on CNN's television program, *Larry King Live*. An outspoken critic of the agreement, Perot had claimed that NAFTA would lead to a "giant sucking sound" of American jobs being lost to Mexico. Gore sought to defend the agreement on behalf of the Clinton administration, which was pushing a reluctant Congress to approve it.

In the opening minutes of the debate, Perot casually suggested imposing a "social tariff" on imports from Mexico to offset that country's lower wages. Gore pounced and brought out a framed picture of two men. "This is a picture of Mr. Smoot and Mr. Hawley," the vice president stated. "They look like pretty good fellas." He went on to explain that "they sounded reasonable at the time" and that a lot of people believed them in 1930 when they said that increasing tariffs on imports would help protect workers. Congress passed the Smoot-Hawley tariff bill and, Gore noted solemnly, it "was one of the principal causes, many economists say the principal cause, of the Great Depression in this country and around the world." He handed the picture to Perot and said, "Now I framed this so you can put it on your wall if you want to." Perot received the picture coolly and put it face down on the desk. "We are talking [about] two totally different, unrelated situations," he insisted.

Soon after the debate, Congress approved NAFTA. According to later polling, Gore's spirited defense helped swing public opinion to view the agreement more favorably. His dramatic invocation of Smoot and Hawley, more than sixty years after the enactment of their notorious tariff act, reminded viewers of the long-standing association of protectionism, a collapse in world trade, and the Great Depression in the early 1930s. Ever since then, the ghosts of Smoot and Hawley have stood in the way of anyone arguing for higher trade barriers. Almost singlehandedly, these two men made the term "protectionist" an insult rather than a compliment.

Who were Smoot and Hawley? And why do we still remember what they did more than eighty years later?

Reed Smoot was a Republican Senator from Utah and chairman of the Senate Finance Committee from 1923 to 1933. Willis Hawley was a Republican member of the House of Representatives from Oregon and chairman of the House Ways and Means Committee from 1928 to 1931. These two committees were charged with craft-

Vice President Al Gore shows a picture of Hawley and Smoot during the NAFTA Debate with Ross Perot on CNN's *Larry King Live* in 1993. Source: Photo courtesy of CNN © 1993.

ing tariff legislation, and in 1929 and 1930, Smoot and Hawley were responsible for ushering through Congress the bill that bears their name.[1] President Herbert Hoover signed it into law on June 17, 1930.

We still remember the Smoot-Hawley tariff because it ranks among the most infamous pieces of congressional legislation of the twentieth century. Although imports were not surging into the country or causing any great problem for the economy, Congress raised tariffs on imported goods with the intention of protecting farmers and

---

[1] Because the Constitution provides that revenue measures must originate in the House before going to the Senate, tariff legislation was often named for the Ways and Means Committee chair first and the Senate Finance Committee chair second. This implies that the legislation should be known as the Hawley-Smoot tariff, but Smoot played such a large role in its passage that contemporaries began to refer to it as the Smoot-Hawley tariff.

manufacturers from what little foreign competition they faced. In doing so, they did not follow any economic logic or consider the interests of consumers and exporters who would be harmed by the tariffs. Instead, they engaged in the most blatant form of pork-barrel politics, catering to the demands of special interests that wanted to limit imports. Not surprisingly, several foreign countries retaliated by imposing duties on U.S. exports. These trade restrictions spread just as the world economy was beginning to sink into a depression. The contribution of the Smoot-Hawley tariff to the collapse of trade and the Great Depression of the 1930s has been debated ever since.

As one contemporary observer wrote, the Smoot-Hawley tariff "has doubtless occasioned more comment, more controversy, more vituperation in the national as well as in the international sphere than any other tariff measure in history" (Jones 1934, 1). Most of the commentary has been highly critical. "The most disastrous single mistake any U.S. president has made in international relations was Herbert Hoover's signing of the Smoot-Hawley Tariff Act into law in June 1930," Harvard economist Richard Cooper (1987, 291) has argued. "The sharp increase in U.S. tariffs, the apparent indifference of the U.S. authorities to the implications of their actions for foreigners and the foreign retaliation that quickly followed, as threatened, helped convert what would have been otherwise a normal economic downturn into a major world depression." The noted British civil servant Sir Arthur Salter (1932, 173) went so far as to say that the Smoot-Hawley tariff "was a turning point in world history" for its role in unleashing the protectionism that destroyed world trade in the 1930s. The distinguished historian Allan Nevins (1950, 142) agreed that the tariff act "marked a great turning point in the history of the time," calling it an "ill-timed explosion of economic nationalism."

Others have sought to exonerate Smoot and Hawley, arguing that they were not responsible for the economic disasters of the early 1930s. "That the legend of Smoot-Hawley endures and continues to influence the trade policy debate is a tribute to the public relations skills of partisans and ideologues with an agenda," writes Alfred Eckes (1995, 139), a former chairman of the U.S. International Trade Commission. Those partisans and ideologues "successfully transformed a molehill into a mountain." Conservative commentator Pat Buchanan (1998, 247, 250) contends that "not one of the charges against Smoot-Hawley stands up" and the higher tariff "had an imperceptible effect even on trade, let alone on a national economy of which foreign trade was but a tiny fraction."

But those are minority views. Whether deserved or not, Smoot and Hawley have become synonymous with an avalanche of protectionism that led to the collapse of world trade and the Great Depression. Because of the controversy that surrounded its passage and the catastrophe that followed in its wake, it is easy to resort to hyperbole when discussing the Smoot-Hawley tariff. In a book on American history, humorist Dave Barry (1990, 116) has an extended riff on the Smoot-Hawley tariff as "the most terrible and destructive event in the history of Mankind."

Smoot and Hawley have even become cultural icons, their names resonating far beyond the world of policy wonks. A classic scene from the 1986 movie, *Ferris Bueller's Day Off*, illustrates the extent to which the Smoot-Hawley tariff has become part of the public vocabulary. In the movie, actor Ben Stein plays a high school teacher who drones on in a slow monotone:

> In 1930, the Republican-controlled House of Representatives, in an effort to alleviate the effects of the—anyone? anyone?—the Great Depression, passed the—anyone? anyone?— the tariff bill, the Hawley-Smoot Tariff Act which—anyone? raised or lowered?—raised tariffs in an effort to collect more revenue for the federal government. Did it work? Anyone? Anyone know the effects? It did not work, and the United States sank deeper into the Great Depression.

Stein's memorable portrayal of the quintessential boring high school teacher introduced Smoot and Hawley to a new generation of young people.[2]

To this day, presidents, members of Congress, journalists, and economists speak of the "lessons" of protectionism and Smoot-Hawley. But what are those lessons? One can find those who would argue that the Smoot-Hawley tariff was responsible for the collapse of world trade, or that it had nothing to do with it. One can find claims that the Smoot-Hawley tariff caused the Great Depression, or

---

[2] Stein (2007) later noted that the lines from that scene were ad-libbed. Indeed, it is hard to imagine a Hollywood scriptwriter setting out to pen a few sentences about an obscure tariff bill written long ago, whereas Stein—the son of the distinguished economist Herbert Stein—was familiar with the issue and able to tell the basic story off the top of his head.

that it had nothing to do with it. Where does the truth lie and what should we remember about it?

This book examines the Smoot-Hawley tariff and its consequences. Chapter 1 focuses on the long and politically divisive passage of the Smoot-Hawley tariff through Congress. The popular perception is that Congress enacted a higher tariff because it caved in to the demands of special interest groups. In fact, the tariff did not originate in response to demands by politically powerful industries facing competition from imports, but was offered up by Republican politicians who wanted to appease farmers during the presidential election campaign in 1928. The tariff was initiated near a business cycle peak when business was good, not in the midst of the Depression, and it was poorly suited to help farmers, many of whom depended on exports to foreign markets. Of course, the manner in which Congress handled the tariff gave rise to its association with special interest lobbying and logrolling (vote trading among members of Congress), a perception that is wholly accurate.

Chapter 2 addresses the economic effects of the tariff. The popular perception is that the Smoot-Hawley tariff raised import duties to record levels and helped cause the Great Depression. In fact, the legislated tariff increase was much smaller than commonly imagined, although it still managed to erase 15 percent of America's imports of dutiable goods upon impact. For reasons that will be explained, it was the deflation of prices that accompanied the Great Depression that pushed the tariff to near record levels, restricting trade even more. Furthermore, contrary to what Vice President Gore argued during the NAFTA debate, most economic historians do not believe that the Smoot-Hawley tariff played a large role in the macroeconomic contraction experienced during the Depression. Instead, a series of monetary and financial shocks pushed the economy into a downward spiral, with the tariff playing a secondary role.

Chapter 3 examines at the international reaction to the Smoot-Hawley tariff. The popular perception is that the tariff backfired by triggering retaliation against U.S. exports and the spread of trade blocs that discriminated against the United States, inflicting long-term damage for U.S. commercial and foreign policy interests. In fact, this perception is largely accurate. While countries did not broadcast that they were retaliating against the United States for imposing the tariff, the nature and timing of the measures they took strongly suggest that was the primary motivation. A month after the Smoot-Hawley tariff was imposed, a pro-American Liberal government in Canada lost a general election to the pro-British Conservatives, who erected trade barriers designed to shift Canada's imports from the United States to Britain. Other countries discriminated against U.S. exports as well, and the nation's share of world trade fell sharply. The higher sugar duties even helped spark a revolution in Cuba that overthrew a regime that had been friendly to the United States.

Chapter 4 assesses the aftermath and legacy of the Smoot-Hawley tariff. Smoot-Hawley gave congressional trade policy making a bad name that persists to this day. Those who enacted it promised economic growth and prosperity, but it was followed instead by plummeting exports and depression. The Tariff Act of 1930, the formal name of the Smoot-Hawley tariff, was the last general tariff revision undertaken by Congress. Four years later, Congress ushered in a new era of U.S. trade policy by delegating power to the president to negotiate agreements with other countries to reduce tariffs. This approach gave us our current system, embodied in the General Agreement on Tariffs and Trade (GATT) and its successor, the World Trade Organization (WTO). Yet the lessons of Smoot-Hawley continue to be debated whenever trade policy issues rise to the top of the national agenda.

Chapter 1
Domestic Politics

To UNDERSTAND THE FACTORS that gave rise to the Smoot-Hawley tariff, we need to understand the process by which Congress handled tariff revisions and the political forces at work in the late 1920s.

The U.S. Constitution gives Congress the authority to levy duties on imports. From the very beginning, the use of this power was controversial. Throughout the nineteenth century, the debate centered on whether tariffs should be levied to raise revenue for the federal government, or to protect domestic industries from foreign competition as well. With the introduction of the income tax in 1913, tariffs were no longer a major source of government revenue.[1] As a result, Congress began to use tariffs mainly to protect domestic industries from imports.

[1] After the Civil War, import duties raised about half of the revenue collected by the federal government. Following the introduction of the income tax, import duties generated less than 10 percent of the government's revenue.

The only question was whether a domestic industry's desire to stop foreign competition should take precedence over the interests of consumers and exporters in having an open market for imported goods.

In confronting this question, Congress ran up against deeply rooted regional differences on matters of trade policy. For most of the nineteenth century and into the twentieth, proponents of high protective tariffs came from the North, where manufacturing industries faced competition from imports. Opponents of high tariffs came from the South, where cotton and tobacco farmers exported their crops to foreign markets. Interests in the Midwest were mixed. Midwestern farmers were consumers of manufactured goods and wanted lower tariffs on industrial goods to promote competition and reduce prices. At the same time, they also wanted high tariffs on agricultural imports that competed with the goods they produced.

The positions of the two main political parties reflected these regional differences. Prior to 1930, Republicans were mainly elected from the North and Midwest and advocated a policy of protectionism, although they sometimes had to accommodate the Midwest's mixed position. Democrats were mainly elected from the South and opposed high tariffs out of concern that trade restrictions would ultimately reduce southern exports. Hence, whenever the Republicans were in power, they voted to impose or maintain high tariffs; whenever the Democrats were in power, they voted to lower tariffs.

Of course, for any particular member of Congress, the economic interests of one's constituents trumped partisan loyalties. A Democrat elected from Pennsylvania or Louisiana would not support the party's low tariff position if it meant allowing more imports of steel or sugar. Similarly, a Republican elected from Wisconsin or Iowa would not support the party's high tariff position if it meant increasing the cost of manufactured products consumed by farmers. As John Sherman (1895, 2: 1128), a Republican senator from Ohio for thirty-seven years after the Civil War, wrote: "It is easy to formulate general principles, but when we come to apply them to the great number of articles named on the tariff list, we find that the interests of their constituents control the action of Senators and Members."

As an institution, Congress was biased in favor of high tariffs because of an asymmetry in the political influence between those that favor reducing imports and those that favor unrestricted imports. As a general matter, domestic producers facing foreign competition are very politically active in advocating restrictions on imports, whereas consumers and exporters who are harmed directly or indirectly by import barriers tend to be politically inactive. This asymmetry in political activism reflects a simple cost-benefit calculation: the benefits of a tariff are highly concentrated on a few producers who are strongly motivated to organize and defend that policy, whereas the costs of tariffs are spread widely among many consumers for whom it does not pay to organize any serious opposition.

This bias was highlighted by political scientist E. E. Schattschneider in his classic study of the Smoot-Hawley tariff, *Politics, Pressures, and the Tariff*, published in 1935. He focused on the public hearings that Congress held before drafting the tariff legislation. Expecting that the economic interests supporting and opposing the tariff legislation would be approximately equal,

Schattschneider (1935, 285) found instead that the pressures exerted upon Congress were "extremely unbalanced. . . . the pressures supporting the tariff are made overwhelming by the fact that the opposition is negligible." Schattschneider (1935, 109) described the highly skewed forces confronting Congress this way: "The primary, positive, offensive activity of domestic producers seeking increased duties almost completely dominated the whole process of legislation. The pressures from this quarter were more aggressive, more powerful, and more fruitful by a wide margin of difference than all of the others combined." In fact, opposition to higher tariffs by consumer groups, exporters, or importers was "usually inconsequential."[2]

What explained the imbalance in political power between those in favor of higher tariffs and those opposed? In Schattschneider's view:

> The political agitation concerning the tariff is profoundly influenced by the fact that, in many instances, the benefits of the legislation to an individual producer are obvious while many of the costs are obscure. The benefits, moreover, are directly associated with a single duty, or at most, a few duties, while costs tend to rise from

[2] Schattschneider also reported that management got almost exclusive representation before Congress, with little participation by labor groups, consumers, and the broader community. He was also amazed by the lack of conflict in formulating tariff legislation. The practice of "reciprocal non-interference" meant that no producer would oppose higher duties for other producers; that is, it is "proper for each to seek duties for himself but improper and unfair to oppose duties sought by others" (1935, 136). If a problem arose, "it is easier to move with the stream by asking for an increase of the duties on the output of his industry than it is to provoke conflicts on a wide front by resisting the series of duties levied against him" (128).

multitudes of them. Benefits are concentrated while costs are distributed. (127–28)

The nature of international trade and the geography of domestic production reinforced Congress's bias in favor of high tariffs. The United States imported a highly diversified set of goods, making it likely that some producers in every state would be competing against imports. For example, wool producers in Ohio and Colorado, steel producers in Pennsylvania and Ohio, glass producers in Pennsylvania and New Jersey, textile producers in Massachusetts and Rhode Island, and many others, all had an interest in reducing foreign competition. This meant that the geographic political base that supported protectionist trade policies, while concentrated in the north, was generally very broad. Meanwhile, U.S. exports were composed of a limited number of goods that were produced in a few specialized regions of the country, such as cotton and tobacco in the Deep South. This meant that the geographic base for supporting open trade policies was relatively narrow.

In addition, members of Congress engaged in logrolling—vote trading—as a way of maintaining high tariffs. For example, a representative from Ohio, whose constituents wanted to stop imports of cheap wool, might agree to vote for a higher tariff on steel to benefit Pennsylvania, or cotton textiles to benefit Massachusetts, if the representatives from those states would vote in favor of a higher tariff on wool. The benefits to the Ohio wool producers from the wool tariff were much more apparent than the higher costs of steel and textile goods to consumers in Ohio. Because this kind of vote trading was a common practice in the halls of Congress, members whose constituents would benefit from lower tariffs found it hard to gain support.

After the Civil War, Congress revised the tariff code about every decade or so. These revisions depended on shifts in political power and the state of the economy. If an election transferred power from one party to another, the newly elected party usually enacted a new schedule of import duties that better served the interests of its constituency. If the economy was doing well, Congress would face little political pressure to change the existing duties, but if the economy was in a recession, the demands for new import restrictions would invariably increase.

These last two factors make it somewhat surprising that Republicans proposed a tariff revision in 1928. Less than six years had passed since they had last altered the tariff code with the Fordney-McCumber tariff in September 1922. Since that time, the Republicans had maintained political control and the economy had been performing well. In fact, the U.S. economy was booming in 1929: during that year, real GDP increased more than 6 percent and the unemployment rate was about 3 percent (Carter and Sutch 2006, series Ca9 and Ba475). Manufacturers were not complaining about surging imports or intensified competition from foreign producers. The nation produced $47 billion in manufactured goods, but imported just $854 million in dutiable manufactured goods. This meant that the import penetration ratio (imports as a percent of domestic consumption) was less than 3 percent. Furthermore, American manufacturers as a whole were much more dependent on exporting to foreign markets than they were threatened by imports: in 1929, about 8 percent of U.S. manufacturing output was exported and the United States enjoyed a $1.4 billion trade surplus in manufactured goods.

In fact, most imports did not affect domestic manufacturers at all. Two-thirds of U.S. imports entered duty-free. They were either consumer goods (such as coffee, tea, and bananas) or raw materials used by industry (such as silk, petroleum, rubber, copper, tin, fertilizer, and cocoa beans) that were either not produced at home or produced in insufficient quantity to meet American demand. The remaining one-third of imports competed with domestically produced products, and consequently they were slapped with high tariffs. Examples include duties of 94 percent on imported sugar, 62 percent on silk goods, 51 percent on wool and wool manufactures, 50 percent on cotton manufactures, 60 percent on glass and pottery, and so on. These tariffs significantly reduced imports and allowed domestic producers in these categories to dominate the U.S. market. Small, high-cost producers always hoped for even higher tariffs to eliminate the residual imports entering the U.S. market and expand their sales. But by and large, the American economy was doing well in the late 1920s, and this prosperity meant that there was no significant political pressure from industry to further limit imports.

Why, then, did the Republicans propose a tariff revision in 1928? The main reason was that another segment of the nation's economy was not doing well: agriculture. The 1920s was an exceptionally difficult decade for American farmers. Foreign demand for U.S. agricultural goods soared during the boom years of World War I, and farm prices doubled between 1915 and 1918. This sparked a wave of land speculation and large investments in machinery and buildings as farmers sought to expand their production capacity. It also pushed farm indebtedness to record levels. When a sharp tightening of monetary and credit conditions led to an unexpected collapse of commodity prices in late 1920 and early 1921, heavily indebted farmers faced a huge financial squeeze. Although manufacturing industries were also slammed by the 1920–21 recession, they quickly bounced back and grew rapidly for the rest of the decade. Agriculture remained in a prolonged and painful slump, with farm income failing to regain its prewar level until 1925 and remaining flat for the rest of the decade.

As the real burden of mortgage debt rose with the fall in commodity prices, farms began to fail in increasing numbers. Foreclosures rose from 3 percent of farms between 1913 and 1920 to 11 percent between 1921 and 1925, and reached an astounding 18 percent of all farms between 1926 and 1929 (Alston 1983). During these years, the entire rural economy suffered from falling farmland prices, mortgage foreclosures, and rural bank failures. The contrast between prosperous industries in the East and struggling farms in the Midwest fueled agrarian resentment against industrial and commercial interests. Manufacturers were protected against foreign competition by high tariffs. Farmers felt that they paid for the tariff through higher prices and now they wanted equal consideration from the politicians in Washington.

With nearly a quarter of the American labor force employed in agriculture, Congress could not ignore the farm sector's plight. Congress began considering new policies to ensure "equality for agriculture" and give equal assistance to farm producers. Because the average tariff on imported agricultural commodities was about half of the average tariff on imported manufactured goods, some thought parity for agriculture could be achieved through a higher tariff on the products that farmers sold or a lower tariff on the goods they purchased. As a result, many agricultural interest groups, represented by such organizations as the National Grange, the American Farm Bureau Federation, and the National Farmers Union, supported the idea of tariff equality.

However, they sought to achieve this mainly through an increase in agricultural tariffs, rather than a decrease in industrial tariffs. "There was practically no direct attack upon the principle of a high tariff by the national farm organizations," notes Conner (1958, 37). "Instead, the basic approach of these groups was an attempt to secure parity in tariff rates with industry. . . . the thinking of organizational leaders was developed within the framework of a high tariff structure, the emphasis being upon raising agricultural rates to obtain parity with industry, rather than upon lowering any or all rates." In fact, farm groups planned to speak out against industrial tariffs only if the tariff on agricultural goods could not be increased to match those on industrial products. The National Grange's threatening slogan was "a tariff for all or a tariff for none."

The big problem with using tariffs to assist agriculture was that it would not help the large number of farmers who produced goods for export. Table 1.1 presents the U.S. exports and imports of agricultural goods by commodity type. The United States was a large net exporter of key crops such as cotton and tobacco, produced in the South, and grains such as wheat, produced in the Midwest: the nation sold one-half of its cotton, one-third of its tobacco, and one-fifth of its wheat and

TABLE 1.1.
U.S. Foreign Trade in Agricultural Products, 1929
(in US$ millions)

	Exports	Imports	Balance
Net exports			
Cotton	$771	$53	+$718
Wheat and other grains	$286	$20	+$266
Tobacco	$146	$54	+$92
Fruits	$136	$59	+$77
Meat	$79	$41	+$38
Net imports			
Dairy products and eggs	$22	$30	−$8
Animals	$2	$21	−$19
Vegetables	$25	$48	−$23
Wool	$1	$87	−$86
Sugar	$18	$229	−$211
Coffee, tea, and beverages	$4	$379	−$375

Source: *Statistical Abstract of the United States* (1931), 675,
574–84.

flour to foreign markets. The price at which these commodities were sold was determined by the world market. Imposing higher duties on the trivial amount of imports of these goods could not provide farmers with any relief because it would have no effect on the prices that farmers received for their crops.

Furthermore, the small amount of these imports did not really compete with domestic producers: long-staple cotton from Egypt was quite different from the cotton produced in the United States, imported hard spring wheat from Canada only affected producers in the border states of the Northwest, and imported tobacco wrappers were completely different from the raw tobacco produced in North Carolina. Some upper midwestern farmers did face limited competition from neighboring Canada, but even here the volume of imports was small. For example, the Smoot-Hawley tariff on eggs was raised from 8 cents to 10 cents a dozen, despite the fact that one egg in 8,500 consumed domestically came from abroad (Canada) and exports of eggs were over one hundred times the amount of imports (Fetter 1933, 418). In the case of vegetables, imports tended to be seasonal and only affect domestic farmers in a limited way.

The major exceptions, products for which imports competed directly with domestic production, were wool and sugar, but these had been protected with high tariffs for many decades. In early 1930, the ad valorem tariff on raw sugar was 99 percent, while the tariff on imported wool was 57 percent.

Many agricultural imports were in categories of goods for which there was either no domestic production, such as coffee and tea, or very limited domestic production, such as various tropical fruits. This did not stop some groups from advocating higher tariffs. They argued that reducing imports would help shift American production into new crops. According to this reasoning, levying stiff duties on imported vegetables and soy beans from Central America would encourage farmers to divert crop land away from cotton and wheat and toward those products. This would reduce the excess supply of the cotton and wheat and raise their price on world markets.

Proponents also argued that higher tariffs would shift consumer demand in a way that would help domestic producers. One agricultural producer recommended imposing a high tariff on bananas, not because the United

States could start producing them but because "the enormous imports of cheap bananas into the United States tend to curtail the domestic consumption of fresh fruits produced in the United States," such as apples (Conner 1958, 40). Thus, high import duties on tropical fruits that the United States did not produce were supposed to encourage consumers to buy more American-produced substitutes, such as apples and oranges. In essence, some farm groups wanted to eliminate the importation of any foreign agricultural products that competed directly or indirectly with American farmers.

Yet the fact remained that a higher tariff would not be very effective in helping the agricultural sector. It would not help the many farmers who produced goods for export, and would provide only limited benefits to those who faced competition from imports. This meant that it was almost certain to be ineffective in raising domestic agricultural prices and reducing farm mortgage debts. This point was widely recognized but not fully appreciated. During the debate over the Fordney-McCumber tariff of 1922, Rep. Carl Hayden (D-AZ) said that including higher tariff rates on agricultural goods

> can be explained in no other way than that they represent an attempt to fool the farmers and swindle the stockmen into the belief that they will get enough benefit out of this bill to fully compensate them for the higher prices that they must pay for all the manufactured goods upon which high protective or even prohibitive duties are levied in this measure. . . . time will soon disclose the utter futility of attempting by a tariff to boost the price of wheat or

corn or short-staple cotton and the numerous other farm and range products where the importations are negligible and the surplus must be sold abroad. (*Congressional Record*, July 14, 1922, 3835, 3840)

The only way Congress could have really helped export-oriented farmers who did not face competition from imports was by directly raising the price they received. This could be done either through domestic price supports, production subsidies, or export subsidies. When the Fordney-McCumber tariff of 1922 failed to provide much relief for agriculture, legislators began considering the idea of increasing farm prices through direct government intervention. Proposals ranged from federal loans and cooperative marketing arrangements to government purchases of farm surpluses at guaranteed prices and export subsidies.

The most noteworthy of such schemes was the McNary-Haugen bill, named for Sen. Charles McNary (R-OR) and Rep. Gilbert Haugen (R-IA). The McNary-Haugen proposal amounted to a domestic price support combined with an export subsidy. The plan called for the creation of a government export corporation that would buy enough agricultural output to raise the domestic price to a government-set target. It would then export any surplus production to foreign consumers at the lower world price. The government would absorb the financial loss either by imposing an equalization tax on farmers or drawing on general revenue. Farm organizations endorsed the McNary-Haugen scheme, but opponents attacked it as unconstitutional, sectional, expensive, and unworkable.

The initial plan was limited to basic commodities such as wheat, wool, cattle, and swine. This political base was too narrow: while the upper Midwest supported it, virtually all eastern states (industry) and the South (cotton) opposed it. The House rejected the proposal in June 1924. Recognizing the need to cultivate additional political support, Midwest farm representatives revised the measure to include cotton among the subsidized crops. In February 1927, a combination of cotton- and corn-belt support led to its passage. The vote was not partisan but regional, pitting the agricultural Midwest and South against the industrial East.

However, President Calvin Coolidge vetoed the bill. He argued that government price-fixing would distort markets by increasing production and decreasing consumption and would be difficult to administer. Coolidge also criticized the bill as sectional because it helped farmers who produced wheat, corn, and cotton and raised hogs, but not those producing oats, barley, and vegetables, or raising beef and poultry. The Republican Party's eastern establishment did not think that the government could or should do much about low farm prices. "Well, farmers never had made much money," Coolidge remarked about the plight of farmers. "I don't believe we can do much about it" (Sundquist 1983, 187).

Frustrated by their failure to obtain any substantive agricultural relief, midwestern members of Congress were determined to strike back at the industrial interests blocking their way. Complaining that government policy favored eastern industry with import tariffs but refused to enact farm subsidies that would help western agriculture, they began to lash out against high tariffs. In December 1927, Sen. William McMaster (R-SD) proposed an immediate, downward revision of the tariff. Rejecting as fraudulent the idea that agricultural tariffs could help farmers, McMaster attacked protection for industry:

> The only way agriculture can win relief is by arousing the industrial East. I want to see the industrial group placed on the defensive just as agriculture has been on the defensive for the last seven years. The West must strike industry where it hurts to get any necessary relief. I know no better way to bring the East to its senses than to tamper with the tariff. The farmer is determined in this. They must either get the benefits of the tariff or they must be relieved of the burdens of the tariff. (Malin 1930, 114–15)

Republican Party leaders rejected any proposal to alter the existing tariff system. Senate Finance Committee chairman Reed Smoot (R-UT) denounced the McMaster resolution:

> This is not the first time in American history that the tariff has been condemned by the West or the South as a plan to enrich the East at the expense of other sections. . . . It is difficult for me to measure the disastrous effect of adopting this resolution by the Senate would have upon business, upon confidence, and upon credit. The very fear of a general lowering of the tariff might precipitate an industrial and business panic. . . . It is a threat, an attack in the dark,

> without a redeeming feature. Its possibilities
> for good are negligible; its possibilities for
> mischief are boundless. (*Congressional Record*,
> January 9, 1928, 1184)

Yet the Republican leadership was overwhelmed by a coalition of midwestern Republicans and southern Democrats in the Senate who helped pass the McMaster resolution by a vote of 54–34. In the House, where the Republican eastern establishment had a stronger grip on power, the proposal was tabled, but only by the narrow margin of 183–164.

Undaunted, farm bloc supporters pressed on, insisting that something had to be done to alleviate the acute distress afflicting agriculture. Congress passed yet another McNary-Haugen bill in early 1928, this time by a wider margin than before. The measure tried to address some of the president's objections, but Coolidge vetoed this bill as well. In a sharply worded message, Coolidge condemned the bill as an unwise price-fixing scheme that would "poison the well-springs of our national spirit" by subsidizing some groups at the expense of others (*Congressional Record*, May 23, 1928, 9524–27).

Defeated again, the midwestern Republicans went back to the drawing board. With the Republican establishment opposed to farm subsidies and unwilling to reduce protective tariffs on manufactured goods, the only solution seemed to be higher tariffs on agricultural goods, as imperfect a solution as that might be.

This lay the groundwork for what would become the Smoot-Hawley tariff. It is ironic that it was set in motion not by industrial lobbyists or the Republican leadership in Congress, but by progressive midwestern Republicans. They would be bitterly dismayed by the end result.

THE PRESIDENTIAL ELECTION OF 1928

The plight of agriculture was an important but not critical issue in the 1928 presidential election campaign. Both parties pledged to help the ailing farm sector but were vague about the potential remedies.[3] The Democrats missed an opportunity to capitalize on agrarian discontent by nominating as their presidential candidate Alfred E. Smith, an anti-prohibition Catholic New Yorker who hardly identified with the concerns of rural America. The Democrats also backed away from their traditional advocacy of low tariffs because they hoped to gain the support of business interests and make inroads into traditional Republican constituencies in the North. To reassure those swing voters, Al Smith vowed that his party, "if entrusted with power, will be opposed to any general tariff bill. . . . No revision of any specific schedule will have the approval of the Democratic party which in any way interferes with the American standard of living and level of wages" (*New York Times*, November 4, 1928, 132).

Meanwhile, the Republicans continued to disappoint farmers by failing to endorse farm subsidies. But to pla-

[3] The Democratic platform promised "to establish and maintain the purchasing power of farm products and the complete economic equality of agriculture" through government credit and marketing assistance. The Republican platform promised to "place the agricultural interests of America on a basis of economic equality with other industries to insure its prosperity and success" and stressed the need for further protection for farmers against foreign competition. See Porter and Johnson (1956, 273, 286).

cate midwestern voters, and in light of the McMaster debate, the party leaders decided they had to offer relief for America's ailing farms through a tariff revision that would focus primarily on restricting imports of agricultural goods. The Republican platform, which was drafted by Sen. Reed Smoot, reaffirmed the party's support for protective tariffs as "a fundamental and essential principle of the economic life of this nation" and as "essential for the continued prosperity of the country." It denied that the protective tariff was a sectional measure, arguing that it was "as vital to American agriculture as it is to American manufacturing." The party insisted that agriculture reaps "large benefits not only directly from the protective duties levied on competitive farm products of foreign origin, but also, indirectly, from the increase in the purchasing power of American workmen employed in industries similarly protected." In other words, they believed that high tariffs on manufactured products supported a growing industrial base that stimulated domestic demand for agricultural goods and thus indirectly helped farmers.

However, in a crucial passage, the platform continued:

> Certain provisions of the present law require revision in the light of changes in the world competitive situation. . . . we realize that there are certain industries which cannot now successfully compete with foreign producers because of lower foreign wages and a lower cost of living abroad, and we pledge the next Republican Congress to an examination and where necessary a revision of these schedules to the end that American labor in these industries may again command the home market,

may maintain its standard of living, and may count upon steady employment in its accustomed field (*New York Times*, June 15, 1928, 8).

In other words, the tariff revision would not be limited to agricultural goods alone, but would include those manufactured goods that could use additional protection.

The platform was a compromise to mollify midwestern Republicans, some of whom had considered breaking off from the Republicans and starting a third party devoted to the interests of agriculture. The carefully worded platform did not pledge that only agricultural tariffs would be increased, but it was understood that agriculture's needs were primary and industry's were secondary.

The Republican presidential nominee, Herbert Hoover, strongly supported the platform. He acknowledged the importance of foreign trade for the nation's economy, but warned that lower tariffs would lead to more imports and lower wages. In accepting the Republican nomination, Hoover argued that "the most urgent economic problem in our nation today is in agriculture. It must be solved if we are to bring prosperity and contentment to one third of our people directly and all of our people indirectly." He insisted that an "adequate tariff is the foundation of farm relief" and pledged to "use my office and influence to give the farmer the full benefit of our historical tariff policy" (*New York Times*, November 4, 1928, 132).

The Tariff Revision Begins

As expected, given the strong economy and the weakness of Al Smith as a presidential candidate, the Republicans crushed the Democrats in the November 1928 election.

Hoover was elected in a landslide and the Republicans increased their majority in Congress.

House Republicans immediately set to work on a tariff bill. In December, Rep. Willis Hawley (R-OR), the likeable but nondescript chairman of the Ways and Means Committee, announced that hearings on a tariff revision would begin in the new year. Consistent with the party platform, there was a general understanding that the main purpose of the revision was to redress the imbalance in the existing tariff and give more protection to agriculture. Still, there was no indication that the revision would be confined exclusively to agricultural goods. And although the Republicans were firmly in power, passage of the new tariff legislation was not a sure thing. In fact, there were important conflicts between the House and Senate, and within the Republican Party, that would make the tariff revision particularly difficult.

Because representation in the House is based on population, the populous eastern states had the most political strength. The "Old Guard" Republican establishment served the manufacturing industries in the East, ranging from shoes and textiles in New England to iron and steel in Pennsylvania. They were not particularly concerned about the farmers in the Midwest. The Republican leadership also ruled the House with a firm grip on power. They tolerated little dissent from the rank-and-file members and enforced restrictive rules on debate to speed legislation through the chamber.

Because representation in the Senate is based on state, the Midwest and far West had much more political power there than in the House. For example, North and South Dakota had twice as many senators as the state of New York, and thinly populated Nevada had as many votes as densely populated Connecticut. In addition, unlike the House, the majority leadership had a weak grip on power and could not control the actions of individual senators, nor could it ram bills through using strict rules that limited debate. Progressive Midwest Republicans, known as "insurgents," often infuriated the Republican leadership by voting against the party line. Led by Senators William Borah (R-ID), Robert M. La Follette, Jr. (R-WI), and George W. Norris (R-NE), they resented the party's Old Guard establishment and blamed it for having consistently tilted the tariff schedule in favor of eastern industrial producers and against western agricultural and raw materials producers. About a dozen strong, the insurgents were numerous enough to join forces with the Senate Democrats, who also represented rural, agricultural states. Together, they could pose a serious threat to the Old Guard's control of the chamber.

From January 7 to February 27, 1929, the Ways and Means Committee held hearings on the tariff revision. The committee reviewed the tariff code, schedule by schedule, paragraph by paragraph. There were fifteen schedules to the tariff code, each dealing with a different set of goods: chemicals; earthenware; metals; wood; sugar; tobacco; agricultural products; beverages; cotton manufactures; flax, hemp, and jute; wool; silk; rayon; paper and books; and sundries. The committee started with chemicals and ended with sundries. In all, the committee heard statements from 1,100 individuals in what came to 10,684 pages of testimony published in eighteen volumes. Often working well into the evening, they listened and questioned producers from around the nation who had a stake in each of the nearly three thousand enumerated goods. About 95 percent of those testifying asked

Willis Hawley and Reed Smoot in front of the Capitol. Source: Library of Congress (National Photo Company).

that the current import duties be raised or, at the very least, maintained.

The hearings were tedious and the level of detail was excruciating. For example, on the first day the committee heard from Dr. F. J. Zinsher, representing Zinscher & Co. with an interest in tannic acid; from Col. W. S. Weeks, representing Calco Chemical Works with an interest in nitric acid; from A. Kochs, representing Victor Chemical Works with an interest in oxalic acid; and so forth. A few weeks later, the National Kraut Packers' Association called for an increase in the duty on kraut from 30 percent to 50 percent and that on cabbage from 25 percent to one-half cent per pound. The New York State Grain and Hay Dealers' Association made a plea for the "humble buckwheat industry" and asked for an increase in the buckwheat tariff from 10 cents to 30 cents per hundredweight. A small firm in Maine requested that the duty on canned sardines be raised from 30 percent to 50 percent, while another from Ohio asked that the tariff on imported goldfish be increased to 35 percent.

As in previous revisions, large firms did not participate in the hearings very much because the tariff was not a major issue for them. They served the national market and they tended to be modern and efficient. They were unconcerned about foreign competition and often exported their goods to foreign markets. Instead, most of the testimony came from small- and medium-sized producers who served local markets and struggled to survive. One report of the hearings noted:

> Hugeness of demands, especially as put forth during the first three weeks of the hearings, probably chilled the ardor which most committee members seemed to have had at the start for complete tariff revision. The most of these demands were accompanied by claims of unemployment, lost earnings, receding profits, and curtailment of operations which the committee obviously soon found hard of acceptance in full form. Moreover, in a majority of cases and ones

where the most direful plaints were uttered, it
was admitted that importations constitute only
fragments of domestic consumption. (*New York
Times*, February 17, 1929, 50)

The rare conflict between producers of intermediate
goods and final goods occasionally enlivened the lengthy
sessions. Laundry soap manufacturers opposed an increase in the tariff on oils and fats because it would increase their costs and drive up soap prices. The boot and
shoe industry wanted to keep hides on the duty-free list,
while ranchers wanted them subject to duties. Dairymen
demanded higher tariffs on casein, a milk by-product, but
that was opposed by coated paper manufacturers, who
used it in their production process. Such conflicts were
usually resolved by offering higher tariffs to both sides.

On March 4, 1929, a few days after the committee
hearings had concluded, President Hoover delivered his
inaugural address. Hoover (1974, 75) stated that "action
upon some of the proposals upon which the Republican
Party was returned to power, particularly further agricultural relief and limited changes in the tariff, cannot in justice to our farmers, our labor, and our manufacturers be
postponed." He called for a special session of Congress
to expedite action on these matters, something William
Borah had pressed him to do, given the severity of agriculture's plight.

The special session opened on April 15, 1929. The next
day, the president sent a message to Congress setting out
his views on the prospective tariff legislation. Hoover
(1974, 79) called for "an effective tariff upon agricultural
products that will compensate the farmer's higher costs
and higher standards of living." The president did not

think that Congress should rewrite the entire 1922 tariff, but simply raise rates on agricultural goods and adjust a few others as circumstances dictated. With respect to non-agricultural duties, Hoover wrote: "It would seem to me that the test of necessity for [tariff] revision is . . . whether there has been a substantial slackening of activity in the industry during the past few years, and a consequent decrease of employment." Because the economy had been doing well, most people thought these changes would be few in number. The president also issued this caution: "In determining changes in our tariff we must not fail to take into account the broad interests of the country as a whole, and such interests include our trade relations with other countries. It is obviously unwise protection which sacrifices a greater amount of employment in exports to gain a less amount of employment from imports."

When Hoover sent this message, the Republican members of the Ways and Means Committee were in secret deliberations to finalize the precise rates of duty in their bill. Once again, the level of detail was mind-boggling. For example, in the final legislation, paragraph 390 of Schedule 3 (Metals, and manufactures of) read: "Bottle caps of metal, collapsible tubes, and sprinkler tops, if not decorated, colored, waxed, lacquered, enameled, lithographed, electroplated, or embossed in color, 30 per centum ad valorem; if decorated, colored, waxed, lacquered, enameled, lithographed, electroplated, or embossed in color, 45 per centum ad valorem." Paragraph 8 of Schedule 1 (Chemicals, oil, and paints) read: "Antimony: Oxide, 2 cents per pound; tartar emetic or potassium-antimony tartrate, 6 cents per pound; sulphides and other antimony salts and compounds, not specifically provided for, 1 cent per pound and 25 per centum ad valorem." The tariff code consisted of nearly two hundred pages of such detail.

This closed-door process of determining the proposed rates gave the advantage to well-connected insiders. Subcommittees on each schedule in the tariff code were headed by members of the Committee with relevant interests, so that a representative from Massachusetts chaired the subcommittee on the cotton manufactures schedule, a representative from Pennsylvania headed the subcommittee on the iron and steel schedule, and so forth. The process involved much horse-trading between the members of the committee and the Republican leadership over the structure of the rates, and it is doubtful that the president's advice mattered much to them. In general, Congress felt that it should write the laws free from executive interference, and it did not always appreciate receiving missives from the president.

On May 9, 1929, Hawley unveiled the result to the House. The proposed bill increased 845 rates and decreased 82 rates from the 2,683 enumerated rates in the existing 1922 tariff act. The committee report, written by the Republican majority, stated that "the readjustments are justified by existing differences in competitive conditions, and necessary for the welfare of all interested in the changes made, and that they will maintain and promote the general welfare" (House Report No. 7, 71st Congress, 1st Session, 11). On the House floor, Hawley noted that "we all enjoy the American standard of living which has been created and is maintained by the protective tariff." When asked what underlying principle guided the rate changes, Hawley replied: "Wherever the evidence indicates and from our information proves that American industry was suffering from a competitive condition to its disadvantage in competition with the foreign producer or with foreign imports, we adjusted that rate to meet the competitive conditions." This meant that, for domestic industries, "whatever rate was necessary for their protection should be written" (*Congressional Record*, May 9, 1929, 1073–74).

Yet, despite the Republicans' insistence that the revised tariff would primarily help agriculture, the bill increased duties on manufactured goods more than it increased duties on agricultural goods. This imbalance was viewed as a step away from "tariff equality" and rekindled tensions between eastern Republicans and the midwestern progressives.[4] Midwestern Republicans were even more disappointed that the bill did not include an export debenture program. Developed as an alternative to the McNary-Haugen plan, the debenture scheme was effectively an export subsidy designed to help the many export-oriented farmers who, as we have seen, would not benefit from import tariffs. Under the plan, an exporter of farm goods would receive a debenture (certificate) equal to half of the value of the import tariff on the good. For example, if the tariff on wheat was 42 cents per bushel, a farmer would receive a certificate for 21 cents for every bushel of wheat exported. Even if the tariff did not really protect wheat farmers from imports because the United States

[4] Eastern Republicans supported higher tariffs on industrial goods but believed that imports of raw materials and foodstuffs were not "detrimental" and therefore did not need greater protection; indeed, they argued that taxes on raw materials and foodstuffs were harmful because they raised the costs of production and the cost of living. For example, Fiorello H. LaGuardia (R-NY) strongly supported tariffs on manufactured goods to "protect American labor," but he opposed higher tariffs on agricultural goods such as sugar and butter as cutting into the budgets of urban consumers. As an example, he denounced a higher duty on potatoes as "nothing but downright larceny" (*Congressional Record*, May 25, 1929, 1951).

exported much of its crop, the debenture would be valuable to the farmer. The certificate was like cash and could be sold at something close to face value to importers, who could use it to pay import duties. Still, the Republican leadership strongly opposed any subsidies for farmers and refused to include such a provision in the tariff bill.

As the House concluded its consideration of the tariff, separate farm relief legislation had already sped through Congress. The Agricultural Marketing Act of 1929 created the Federal Farm Board with a fund of $500 million to make loans to cooperative marketing associations owned and controlled by farmers. Hoover sought this measure, which was intended to help farmers by providing an initial advance of capital without explicit government subsidies. An export debenture system was initially included in the House version, but after waffling, Hoover (1974, 86–100) finally came out strongly against it, saying that it "would bring disaster to the American farm." Hoover opposed the debenture on the grounds that it would promote overproduction and further depress prices, trigger foreign retaliation against the subsidized exports that would erase any benefit to farmers, and cost the Treasury an estimated $200 million. Bowing to the president's demands, the House stripped the debenture from the farm relief bill.

Meanwhile, the minority Democrats strongly opposed the Hawley bill. Although the party's northern leadership had softened its opposition to protectionism during the presidential election, House Democrats were dominated by members from the South, where anti-tariff sentiment still ran high. Rep. Cordell Hull (D-TN), who wrote the Ways and Means Committee minority report, criticized the Republican approach to tariff policy. He said that it allowed excessive or prohibitive rates to be dictated by lobbyists for powerful special interest groups and ensured that "the old and worst type of logrolling and political pressure of conflicting interests will be continued" (House Report No. 7, Part 2, 71st Congress, 1st Session, 2). On the House floor, Hull attacked the bill with the standard Democratic complaint that import tariffs would fail to help the majority of American farmers who depended on export markets. He argued that "existing prohibitive tariffs injure the American farmer first, by increasing his production costs; second, his living costs; third, his transportation costs; fourth, by decreasing his foreign markets and exports; and fifth, by decreasing his property values due to surplus congestion" (*Congressional Record*, May 28, 1929, 2127).

But Hull did not speak for all Democrats. Some Democrats did not oppose the entire system of protection as much as they wanted a different distribution of its benefits, namely, more protection for agriculture and less protection for industry, a view shared by midwestern Republicans. As Rep. John N. Garner (D-TX) stated: "I believe in the principle of protection. But I believe protection should be equally distributed; that the farmers of the South and West are as much entitled to the benefits of tariff protection as the manufacturers of New England and Pennsylvania." Unfortunately, he complained, "every effort to lower industrial rates to a point of parity with agricultural rates has met the opposition of that small coterie of Republican leaders who have controlled the destinies of this bill ... Defeat of the export debenture killed the last hope of over 80 percent of American farmers to secure any substantial relief through the tariff" (*Congressional Record*, June 14, 1930, 10762).

President Hoover was also privately dissatisfied with the imbalance in the House bill. He met with House Republicans to request that they modify it by increasing agricultural tariffs and reducing industrial tariffs in line with his campaign pledge. "Chairman Hawley supported me, but the older protectionists under the leadership of Speaker Nicholas Longworth were discontented," Hoover recalled in his memoirs (1952, 293).

The president also insisted that the bill continue the "flexible tariff" authority that allowed the executive branch to modify import duties on its own. First enacted as a part of the Fordney-McCumber tariff of 1922, the flexible tariff provision permitted the president to adjust an import duty by as much as 50 percent (up or down) if an investigation by the Tariff Commission found that the tariff did not equalize the differences in costs of production between the United States and foreign countries. Progressives had championed this approach in the 1910s in the hopes that an impartial body could help "take the tariff out of politics" and temper many of the extreme duties that Congress had slipped into the tariff schedule. As Hoover (1952, 292–93) later wrote in his memoirs:

> I believed that the only way to get the tariff out of Congressional logrolling was through empowering this bipartisan commission to adjust the different rates on dutiable goods upon the basis of differences in cost of production at home and abroad, and to make these readjustments after objective examination and public hearings. . . . Any tariff passed by the logrolling process, inevitable in the Congress, is bound to be very bad in spots. The object of the flexible

tariff was to secure, in addition to more equitable rates, a hope that Congressional tariff
making could be ended.

The president's views had a limited effect on the House
Republican leaders. They had already included the flexible tariff provision. Yet, in order to satisfy Republicans
from western states, they agreed to some additional increases in agricultural duties, such as on butter, onions,
and potatoes, and moved hides off of the duty-free list
(while giving a compensatory increase to the duty on
boots and shoes). Once the Republican caucus was satisfied, the party's leadership followed the standard practice
of limiting the House debate on the Hawley bill and giving priority to amendments proposed by the Ways and
Means Committee. This ensured that those who wrote
the bill had a virtual lock on any changes to it, effectively
preventing Democrats and progressive Republicans from
altering its contents.

Given the large Republican majority in the House,
passage of the tariff bill was a foregone conclusion. On
May 28, 1929, after several days of debate, the House
approved the tariff bill by a party-line vote of 264–147;
95 percent of Republicans voted in favor and 87 percent
of Democrats voted against. More northern Democrats
voted for the bill than midwestern Republicans voted
against it.[5]

[5] The *New York Times* reported: "Whether it was because of the heat of the
day or weariness superinduced by long hours of discussion, the enthusiasm that
usually marks the conclusion of labors on a big party measure was lacking in the
House chamber on this occasion. There was only a feeble cheer on the Republican side as Speaker Longworth announced the passage of the bill, while the
Democrats, overwhelmed by superior numbers, moved sullenly in their seats"
(May 29, 1929, 1).

As figure 1.1 shows, Republicans from the Northeast, industrial Midwest, and far West supported the House bill, with only a few "corn belt" progressives from Minnesota, Iowa, South Dakota, and Nebraska dissenting. Democrats from the South uniformly opposed the measure, except those from Florida and Louisiana, who wanted to ensure that imports of sugar remained highly taxed.

Empirical studies of the House vote on the Hawley bill have sought to determine some of the underlying political and economic factors behind the legislation. Eichengreen (1989) hypothesized that a coalition of northern farmers and light industries drove the passage of Smoot-Hawley, although he did not formally investigate these influences. In a statistical analysis of the House vote, Callahan, McDonald, and O'Brien (1994) fail to uncover any evidence of such a coalition. Constructing indices of the amount of heavy and light manufacturing in each representative's district and indicators for Canadian border states, they predicted each representative's vote by these economic interests, state unemployment, political party, and a measure of each representative's ideology. They found that only unemployment and political party had a statistically or economically meaningful effect on a representative's vote.

Smoot and the Senate

Having passed the House, the tariff bill was then referred to the Senate Finance Committee, chaired by Reed Smoot of Utah. Smoot was widely recognized as an exceptionally capable and indefatigable legislator who was unquestionably the most knowledgeable member of Congress about the details of the tariff schedule. He

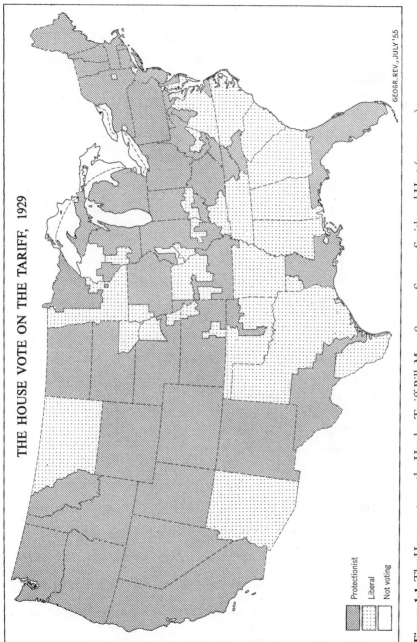

THE HOUSE VOTE ON THE TARIFF, 1929

GEOGR. REV., JULY '55

Protectionist
Liberal
Not voting

Figure 1.1. The House vote on the Hawley Tariff Bill, May 28, 1929. Source: Smith and Hart (1955, 330).

was also a committed protectionist with no misgivings or second thoughts about the policy. As a matter of principle, he opposed almost any reduction in tariff rates.[6] An apostle in the Mormon church, Smoot was known as the "apostle of protection" and "the sugar senator" because of his staunch defense of Utah's sugar beet industry. As one senator put it:

> Of course the Senator from Utah would say that in some instances the rates are not high enough. I can state the rate which he has in mind, and even if it were double the rate now provided in the bill, it would not be high enough for him. He dreams of sugar, he tastes sugar, he sees sugar morning, evening, and night. (*Congressional Record*, September 19, 1922, 12906)

The humorist Will Rogers once quipped: "120,000,000 of us eat it, and exactly 1,231 who raise it. But Reed has dedicated his entire political career to make sugar not only sweet but dear to the 120,000,000" (Rogers 1978, 51).

Smoot was also ambitious. He worked very hard and with great pride on the Payne-Aldrich Tariff of 1909 and the Fordney-McCumber Tariff of 1922, but received little credit. Now Smoot wanted his name attached to a great piece of tariff legislation. His biographer even suggests

---

[6] His biographer wrote, "there is no evidence that any apparent fact, any argument, any introspection even faintly disturbed the certainty of his knowledge" and belief in the benefits of protectionism, or that weakened his unalterable opposition to any reduction (Merrill 1990, 288). In Frank Taussig's (1930, 184) view, Smoot "was not only an out-and-out protectionist of the most intolerant stamp, but was strongly interested in his own region and its own product, beet sugar; not regarded as an impartial or disinterested person, and not entitled to be so regarded."

that this pride may have led him to want something more than a "limited" tariff revision so that his name would be affixed to something of lasting significance.[7] After the Tariff Act of 1930 was passed, he proudly took to calling it the Smoot-Hawley act, instead of the standard designation as Hawley-Smoot, putting his name first to highlight his leading role in the legislation.

As already mentioned, because representation in the Senate is based on state rather than population, the Midwest and West had far greater political power in the Senate than in the House, which was dominated by the populous East. In the House, the majority leadership could limit floor debate, whip the rank and file into line, and ram a bill through. In the Senate, power is much more decentralized because there are fewer legislators. Individual senators have a great deal of power and Senate rules also give party leaders much less control over a bill once it reaches the floor. As a result, the Senate was primed for a battle between the industrial east and the agricultural west in a way that the House had managed to avoid.

From the start, Republican "insurgents" in the Senate—the term given to the Midwestern progressive Republicans who bucked the party line—were outraged by the House bill. They believed that the House had disregarded Hoover's expressed desire for a "limited" revision of the tariff and had completely ignored farm interests. The main leader of the insurgents, William Borah of

[7] "Unquestionably, he wanted his name . . . on one of the great tariff acts," Merrill (1990, 331) writes, because "to Smoot it was an honor paralleled only by the presidency. Moving up a few agricultural commodity rates would certainly not constitute a tariff act. It is not suggested that this senatorial ambition was the primary force in that symbol of Republican ineptitude, the Smoot-Hawley Act, but it was a reasonably significant secondary factor."

THE PRESIDENT'S ADVICE TO THE TARIFF-MAKER
By Berryman, in the *Evening Star* (Washington, D. C.)

Source: *Washington Evening Star*

Idaho, immediately proposed that the Finance Committee be restricted to considering revisions only to the agricultural schedules of the tariff, keeping industrial tariffs at their existing level. As Borah put it:

> The real fight here is between the agricultural interests and the industrial interests. We feel that we are fighting for equality; that that equality is constantly removed by the fact that duties are substantially increased upon the things we have to buy, even though they may be increased to some extent upon the things we have to sell. (*Congressional Record*, September 26, 1929, 3971)

On June 17, 1929, the Borah resolution was defeated by a single vote of 39–38. Republicans voted 32–13 against it, while Democrats voted 25–7 in favor. Even though the measure failed to pass, the vote clearly demonstrated the strength of the bipartisan "coalition" of midwestern Republicans and southern Democrats that represented farm interests.

The Senate Finance Committee held hearings on the bill from June 12 to July 18. The Committee heard from 1,004 witnesses in testimony that ran 8,618 printed pages in eighteen volumes. Once again, representatives of numerous producer interests appeared before a congressional committee to advocate that higher tariffs be imposed on competing imported goods. (One volume was devoted to protests from foreign countries, an issue that will be considered in chapter 3.)

Republicans on the Finance Committee then met in secret from the end of July through August to determine the adjustments they would make to the House bill. In early September, the Finance Committee reported a bill that tempered some of the increases in industrial rates and padded some of the agricultural rates; in all, they increased 177 rates of duty and decreased 254 rates from the House version. In keeping with President Hoover's wishes, an export debenture was not included, while flexible tariff authority was granted to the president.

In presenting the bill to the Senate, Smoot knew that a big battle was brewing. As a result, he warned: "The people elected a Republican President and Congress in order that a readjustment of the tariff might be in the hands of the friends of protection. If that mandate is rejected and defeated by a group or section of that country, the people will know where to place the blame." He accused

Sen. Reed Smoot is at the head of the table as the Senate Finance Committee meets on July 11, 1929, to discuss the tariff bill. Source: Corbis, © Bettmann/CORBIS.

Democrats of being "aided by sectional forces boding no good to the country" and "abetted by groups of internationalists who are willing to betray American interest and surrender the spirit of nationalism" (*Congressional Record*, September 12, 1929, 3549).

Sen. Furnifold Simmons (D-NC) led the Democratic attack on the tariff bill, calling it "indefensible" and a violation of the campaign pledge to help farmers. "Instead of removing, as promised, the tariff discriminations against agriculture, it greatly increases and extends those discriminations, and because for every dollar it gives to the farmer, it takes from him several dollars in the increased cost of his purchases," he exclaimed (*Congressional Record,* September 12, 1929, 3542). Simmons rejected the bill as "unsatisfactory" to farmers because duties were being imposed either in cases where imports were negligible or where producers depended on exports to world markets. In the latter case, the price received by farmers on world markets would be unaffected by U.S. duties and hence those duties would fail to help them. "The only way the farmer can secure or hope to secure even approximate equality through tariff legislation is by imposing such duties on his products as will or can be effective and by drastic reduction in the duties imposed upon such industrial products as he does not produce and must of necessity buy for farm, home, and family." He rejected the inclusion of the flexible tariff provision as giving "autocratic discretion and power" to the president and complained that it would be ineffective at reducing rates.

The Republican insurgents joined in the attack. Borah argued that the tariff "does not sufficiently protect agriculture" because the agricultural rates were too low and ineffectual and the rates on industrial goods were too high. He excoriated the high duties on manufactured goods, noting that because "a little over 3 percent of the [manufactured] goods which we consume are imported into the United States," amounting to "practically an embargo against importations." Yet Congress was contemplating raising tariffs, he noted in astonishment. "If we are going to pick out the man who is producing under the most adverse circumstances and take that man's condition and situation as a test of the amount of protection necessary, nothing less than an embargo will suffice," he exclaimed (*Congressional Record,* September 16, 1929, 3649). And he ridiculed agricultural duties, noting that one-fiftieth of 1 percent of the corn used in the country was imported, so raising the duty from 15 cents to 25 cents a bushel would do nothing to raise farm prices.

The Senate then began a long and complicated process of revising the bill. First, from September 1929 until February 1930, the Senate considered the Finance Committee amendments as a "committee of the whole," wherein the entire Senate acted as one large committee. Then, in February and March, the Senate considered individually sponsored amendments to the bill, also acting as a committee of the whole. Finally, in March, the Senate proper considered the bill and could revise it once again. This unusual process meant that the Senate had three opportunities to adjust tariffs up or down in roll call votes.

In September, the Senate began by debating the administrative clauses of the bill. In two votes, the bipartisan coalition defeated the Republican leadership on key provisions. On October 2, the coalition stripped from the president the ability to make changes in import duties under the flexible tariff provision and returned that power to Congress. The vote was 47–42; Republicans voted 38–13 to keep the House provision, while Democrats voted 34–4 to change it. President Hoover had warned the Senate not to take this step, emphasizing the importance of giving the executive branch the authority to adjust rates under the flexible tariff provision.[8] However, progressive

---

[8] In a statement on September 24, 1929, the president argued:

No tariff bill ever enacted has been or ever will be perfect. It will contain injustices. It is beyond the human mind to deal with all of the facts surrounding several thousand commodities under the necessary conditions of legislation and not to make some mistakes and create some injustices. It could not be otherwise. Furthermore, if a perfect tariff bill were enacted

Sen. William Borah from Idaho was leader of the progressive Republican "insurgents" who wanted the tariff revision confined to agricultural goods. Source: Library of Congress (Harris & Ewing Collection).

Republicans and Democrats were disillusioned about the provision's ability to "take the tariff out of politics" and argued that it was unconstitutional to give the president the power to adjust tariff rates. Democrats added the concern that the flexible tariff authority had been used mainly to increase duties during the 1920s.

Then, Sen. George Norris (R-NE) proposed an export debenture (subsidy), something that the House had rejected. Members from farm states insisted that a debenture was the only way to ensure that agricultural exporters could benefit from the tariff system. But Hoover firmly opposed any such plan and eastern Republicans complained it would be a costly measure that could be easily undermined by foreign retaliation or countervailing duties. Yet, on October 19, the coalition added a debenture to the bill by a vote of 42–34; Republicans voted 31–14 against, while Democrats voted 28–3 in favor.

Attention then turned to the tariff rates themselves. In October and November 1929, the coalition seized control of the bill and, in a series of roll call votes, succeeded in slashing tariffs on goods used by farmers, such as coal, lumber, leather, and footwear. They often put rates back to the 1922 level in the name of tariff equality. As Sen. Charles Waterman (R-CO) declared:

the rapidity of our changing economic conditions and the constant shifting of our relations with economic life abroad would render some items in such an act imperfect in some particular within a year. It is proved by a half century of experience that the tariff cannot be reviewed by Congress more than once in 7 or 8 years. It is only a destruction of the principle of the flexible tariff to provide that the Tariff Commission recommendations should be made to Congress for action instead of the Executive. Any person of experience in tariff legislation in the last half century knows perfectly well that Congress cannot reopen single items of the tariff without importing discussion all along the line, without the constant unsettlement of business and the importation of contentions and factious questions to

I am a high protectionist, and any product of
the United States, of the soil or of industry,
which needs any protection whatever in order
to go on and live, I am ready to grant the benefits of protection, no matter how high the rate
may be. But I want to see that so distributed
that every rank in the social strata of American
may get the benefit of its equality. Agriculture
does not get the benefit, and we all know it.
(*Congressional Record*, October 18, 1929, 4671)

The Old Guard watched with dismay as the coalition began cutting down rates, particularly on industrial
goods. Sen. George H. Moses (R-NH) blasted Borah
and his supporters as the "sons of the wild jackass," an
epithet that stuck and became a badge of honor for the
insurgents. After the Senate voted to reduce the tariff on
pig iron from $1.50 to $0.75 per ton, David Reed (R-PA)
criticized the coalition for doing "damage to the stability
and the structure of American industry." (The insurgents
replied that Reed would have been quite happy to put
manganese ore on the free list to assist the steel industry, despite the problems it would have caused for western mining states.) Reed sighed with exasperation: "The

---

the destruction of other important duties by Congress. Congress has literally hundreds of times in the past refused to entertain any amendment
to a tariff except in periods of general revision. . . . The flexible provision
is one of the most progressive steps taken in tariff making in all our history. It is entirely wrong that there shall be no remedy to isolated cases of
injustice that may arise through the failure to adequately protect certain
industries, or to destroy the opportunity to revise duties which may prove
higher than necessary to protect some industries and, therefore, become
onerous upon the public. To force such a situation upon the public for
such long periods is, in my view, economically wrong and is prejudicial to
public interest. (Hoover 1974, 302–3)

coalition has made up its mind to knock out every increase in the industrial rates, and we might as well go ahead and have done with it. Then the bill will go to conference, and the House and the Senate will never agree, but we will at least be rid of it and can go on with our routine business" (*Congressional Record*, November 6, 1929, 5239). But Reed also attacked the insurgents for their hostility toward industrial interests:

> The attitude of the Western states, the Middle Western states in particular, the corn belt so called, is one of extreme ill-will toward the industrial states of the East, particularly ours [Pennsylvania]. You might almost think that we were at war with each other. . . . it was brought out only too clearly that it is not only the intention of their bloc to raise every duty favorable to agriculture, but to keep on beating lower and ever lower every duty on industrial products until the agricultural West and the industrial East are on the same level of prosperity, or, as that means, to pull us down until we are on a level of common misery.

Because of the dissension in the Senate, Reed predicted that "the present bill is dead and all of our effort is wasted." Smoot and other Republican leaders quickly rejected Reed's assessment and insisted that the bill would eventually be passed (*New York Times*, October 28, 1929, 1).

The uncertainty surrounding the Senate's deliberations was a moment for presidential leadership. No one had any idea what the White House thought of the insurgent campaign. Did Hoover want the revision confined to the agricultural schedule, or did he approve of the higher rates on industrial goods as well? Yet the president refused to provide any guidance. A White House statement released on October 31, 1929 read simply: "The President has declined to interfere or express any opinion on the details of rates or any compromise thereof, as it is obvious that, if for no other reason, he could not pretend to have the necessary information in respect to many thousands of commodities which such determination requires" (*New York Times*, November 1, 1929, 1).

Then, on November 9, Smoot shocked the Senate by conceding defeat. Admitting that the Finance Committee had lost control of the bill, he offered to hand it over to the coalition and have a recess for ten days to allow them to rewrite it as they pleased. To expedite the process, he proposed that the Senate would then vote on the coalition's bill without debate, something he could in no way guarantee. He may have been trying to call the coalition's bluff, and in fact Borah and Simmons rejected the offer. A *New York Times* editorial explained why:

> It is a mistake to suppose that the rebellious coalition wants to write a bill of its own. Its chief desire is to destroy the bill of the Senate Finance Committee. If the leaders of the coalition were locked up in a committee room and told not to come out until they had produced a measure satisfactory to all their supporters, they would never come out. If the door was burst open, they would doubtless be found

lying about wounded after bloody rows with each other. (November 11, 1929, 20)[9]

The coalition was an effective critic of the proposed legislation, but it did not have a coherent view of what would constitute a better schedule of duties.

In late November, with its work on the tariff left in an uncertain state, the Senate adjourned for the year.

THE TARIFF AND THE STOCK MARKET

In October 1929, while the Senate was debating the tariff bill, the stock market crashed. Although the crash did not cause the Great Depression, it helped tip the economy into a recession. Christina Romer (1990) argues that the crash created uncertainty about future income among consumers, leading them to delay spending on durable goods and thereby reducing aggregate demand. But, as the next chapter will discuss, the Depression involved much more than simply a reduction in consumer spending. Rather, a series of devastating monetary and financial shocks helped push the economy into a severe depression.

The fact that the October stock market crash coincided with the Senate tariff debate has led some to suggest a link between the two. For example, journalist and supply-side economics proponent Jude Wanniski (1978, 125) has famously stated that "the stock market Crash of 1929 and

---

[9] As the *New York Times* had earlier opined: "To apply to the Senate's attitude toward the tariff bill a paraphrase of what the late Senator John H. Thurston of Nebraska said of President [Theodore] Roosevelt: 'Nobody wants it and everyone is for it.' 'Everyone' means, of course, the Senate and not the American people, among whom there seems to prevail a decided apathy with regard to what the Senate is doing with the tariff" (October 26, 1929, 11).

the Great Depression ensued because of the passage of the Smoot-Hawley Tariff Act of 1930." He argues that in the fall of 1929, it looked like the tariff would worsen the debt position of foreigners. This forced them to liquidate dollar assets, which in turn caused the Federal Reserve to tighten credit to prevent a fall in the dollar. Wanniski tries to tie the day-by-day movements in the stock market in late October to news about the tariff, but the correlation seems implausibly forced. For example, the Dow Jones Industrial average fell 6 percent on Wednesday, October 23. But the only tariff news on that day was the failure of the coalition to reduce the duty on carbide. That hardly seems like a make-or-break situation for the overall economy.[10] The next day the market fell another 2 percent when the Senate was considering the tariff on casein, a product of skim milk used to produce glue. The stock market fell 23 percent on Monday and Tuesday, October 28 and 29, but the only tariff news from Sunday was the statement by Sen. Reed that the tariff bill was dead and the response by Sen. Smoot that it was not. It is hard to believe that this squabbling was sufficient to cause share prices to drop by a quarter in value.

Wanniski argues that the prospect of a high tariff bill passing spooked the forward-looking stock market.[11] But in October 1929, the coalition was generally successful

[10] Charles Kindleberger (1986, 125) dismissed as "farfetched" the view that "the stock market crash of October 24, 1929, was a response to the action of a Senate subcommittee, reported on an interior page of the *New York Times*, in rejecting an attempt of some members to hold down a proposed increase in a tariff on carbide."

[11] If the stock market was reacting in fear of higher tariffs, why didn't the market crash in March 1930 when, as we shall see, the Senate Old Guard reasserted control over the bill and started raising rates? Or in May 1930, when the final political obstacles to the passage of the Smoot-Hawley tariff were finally cleared away and the uncertainty about the tariff legislation was finally

in reducing tariff rates on industrial goods, which raised the likelihood that the bill would in fact be defeated. As Sumner (1992, 303) notes, "it is hard to reconcile Wanniski's views with the widespread contemporaneous interpretation that the four weeks from mid-October to mid-November had been a major setback for the protectionist wing of the Republican party." Alfred Eckes (1998) countered Wanniski by suggesting that the coalition's effort to reduce industrial tariffs may have led to the stock market crash because business wanted higher duties. Although this is also improbable, it is more consistent with the events of October 1929.

In fact, it is unlikely that the debate over the tariff bill had any impact on the overall stock market. The run-up and subsequent crash in stock prices was not broadly based, but almost entirely concentrated in public utilities companies, a sector of the economy perhaps least affected by import duties (Bierman 1998; White 1990a). The great expansion of investment trusts and public utility holding companies, along with the growth of margin buying, all fueled the buying of public utility stocks and drove up their prices. Utility holding companies and investment trusts were highly leveraged and used large amounts of debt and preferred stock to make their purchases. The sector was vulnerable to any bad news regarding utility regulation. In October 1929, the bad news arrived: a series of regulatory decisions that were adverse to the public utilities triggered a decline in the price of utility stocks. Investors who had bought on margin were forced to sell,

---

resolved? The stock market may have been forward looking, but it would have been impossible in October 1929 to foresee these events six to eight months in the future.

leading to panic selling of all stocks. In addition, the Federal Reserve Board had been tightening credit since January 1928 in an effort to rein in surging stock prices, and that effort was bound to succeed at some point.

Economic historian Eugene White (1990b, 173) finds "no evidence to support the view that the Smoot Hawley tariff significantly contributed to the crash." If the tariff was an important factor influencing stock prices, one would expect the stocks of firms in industries affected by trade to move differently from other industries. This did not happen. The stocks of export-oriented industries (petroleum products, automobiles and parts, industrial and electrical machinery, packinghouse products) all fell about the same amount as the overall market average, as did the stocks of import-competing industries (sugar, paper, woolens, fertilizers) and non-tradable industries. And the stock prices of industries producing exported, import-competing, and non-traded goods all declined later when the tariff's passage was assured.

As a result, it is unlikely that the Senate's deliberations over the tariff had much to do with the October 1929 stock market crash.

The Senate Reconvenes

When Congress reconvened in January 1930, the Senate—still acting as a committee of the whole—considered the overall bill, including the Finance Committee amendments to the House bill. At this point, the Senate took further actions to moderate the proposed tariff hikes on manufactured goods. Week after week, the Senate was preoccupied with the wearisome process of debating at length and then voting on such narrow tariff categories as crude and scrap aluminum, shoes, coal tar dyes, woven silk fabrics, calcium carbide, glass rods, and milk cans.

The coalition continued to succeed in reducing rates and struck a direct blow at Smoot when, after six days of debate, the Senate voted to reduce the tariff on raw sugar from $2.20 per hundredweight, as proposed by the Finance Committee, to the 1922 Fordney-McCumber rate of $1.75 per hundredweight. (This was in contrast to the House rate of $2.40.) The voting margins on many commodities were quite narrow, meaning a few defections could change the outcome of the voting. Still, the coalition seemed to have the upper hand.

Finally, on March 4, 1930, the Senate completed consideration of the bill in a committee of the whole. Whereas the House had increased 845 rates and reduced 82 rates from the 1922 tariff, the Senate bill now left 620 rates higher and 202 lower. The legislation then shifted to a third venue, the Senate proper, for further debate and amendment before final passage. Senators could once again offer amendments and request new votes on specific tariff rates, even if precisely the same issue had been considered and voted on just weeks earlier. There was no substantive difference between the Senate considering the bill as a committee of the whole and as the Senate proper, but at this stage the Republican leadership was able to reestablish control over the bill and reverse some of the coalition's reductions in industrial rates. It was able to do so by the classic method of logrolling.

For example, on March 5, the day after it took the bill from the committee of the whole, the Senate reconsidered the sugar duties. Smoot could not allow his humiliating defeat on the sugar tariff to stand. He convinced nine senators to change their vote on the sugar tariff in a vote-trading deal in which greater protection would also be given to lumber, oil, cement, and glass. Less than two months after the Senate had voted to restore the 1922 rate on imported sugar, Smoot succeeded in pushing the rate back up to $2.50 per hundredweight, higher than even the House had proposed. Just days later, the Senate reversed itself again and voted to increase duties on lumber, oil, cement, and glass.

The March 1930 reversals of the coalition's efforts to moderate the tariff rates gave rise to accusations of vote trading based on backroom deals and special interest lobbying. Sen. Robert LaFollette (R-WI) attacked the Senate bill as "the product of a series of deals, conceived in secret, but executed in public with a brazen effrontery that is without parallel in the annals of the Senate. . . . it seems to me that a vote for this bill condones the vote-trading deals by which some of the most unjustifiable rates in the bill were obtained. . . . this Congress has demonstrated how tariff legislation should not be made" (*Congressional Record*, March 24, 1930, 5976–77). Just prior to the vote reconsidering the duty on lumber, David Walsh (D-MA) stated:

> I can not help but say that things have been happening here in recent weeks that have somewhat shaken my confidence in the judgment of the Senate always being reflected upon conscientious conviction. If logrolling, which is the trading of votes, is not here, then some other invisible influence has brought about a shifting of votes and reversals of judgment that is unparalleled in the history of

legislation. There have been some very suspicious circumstances connected with the shifting of votes on many of these items. Indeed, it has been admitted privately that votes have been and will be exchanged on all important items. (*Congressional Record*, March 20, 1930, 5669)

But some senators defended their support for constituent interests, as was evident in this exchange between Sen. Charles Waterman (R-CO) and Sen. Carter Glass (D-VA):

[WATERMAN]: I have stated upon the floor of the Senate, and I have stated in the presence of senators elsewhere, that, by the eternal, I will not vote for a tariff upon the products of another state if the senators from that state vote against protecting the industries of my state, and I stand upon that platform.

[GLASS]: I may have a very defective sense of discrimination, but I am unable to see the difference between a doctrine of that sort and a plain trading in votes.

[WATERMAN]: I do not care what the Senator may call it. . . . I shall practice it as long as I sit here. (*Congressional Record*, March 19, 1930, 5601)

Some members of Congress began to refer to the bill as the "Grundy" tariff after Republican Sen. Joseph Grundy (R-PA). He had been the president of the Pennsylvania

GRUNDY'S MAP OF THE SENATE?
By Fitzpatrick, in the *Post-Dispatch* (St. Louis).

Source: *St. Louis Post-Dispatch* Editorial Cartoon Collection, Courtesy of The State Historical Society of Missouri.

Manufacturers' Association and vice president of the American Tariff League until December 1929, when the governor of Pennsylvania appointed him to an open Senate seat. A major fund raiser for the Hoover campaign in 1928, Grundy worked hard to increase industrial rates after they had been reduced in the committee of the whole. Without apology or embarrassment, Grundy implied that any organization that made campaign contributions was entitled to get its money back in the form of a higher tariff on their products. He aroused additional resentment in the Midwest and West by calling agricultural regions "backward."

In addition to reversing many of the coalition's changes, Smoot also took particular interest in strengthening the ban on the importation of obscene materials, which had been weakened in the committee of the whole. As the *New York Times* reported: "With great feeling the tall, nervous chairman of the Senate Finance Committee, his desk piled high with supposedly racy material, read a carefully prepared speech in which he pleaded with the Senate not to modify the present censorship" (March 18, 1930, 5). The debate focused on what constituted obscene material and even led to a discussion of D. H. Lawrence's *Lady Chatterley's Lover*. Scorning such works, Smoot at one point shouted:

> I want them all kept out, but the Senator from New Mexico does not believe that some of these books are obscene. I do. I think they are not only obscene, but they are damnable. I want to say to the Senators now that a father of a child would never want the child to see this obscene matter. The Senators around me have some few of these books here. They are disgusting. They are beastly, beastly! (*Congressional Record*, March 6, 1930, 5417)

The Senate eventually agreed to the censorship of foreign books, and his fight against pornography led to the classic headline: "Smoot Smites Smut." Ogden Nash's poem "Invocation" poked fun at the scene (1931, 24–26):

> Senator Smoot (Republican, Ut.)
> Is planning a ban on smut.
> Oh rooti-ti-toot for Smoot of Ut.
> And his reverend occiput.
> Smite, Smoot, smite for Ut.,
> Grit your molars and do your dut.,
> Gird up your l__ns, Smite h_p and th_gh,
> We'll all be Kansas By and by.

Another verse read:

> Senator Smoot is an institute
> Not to be bribed with pelf;
> He guards our homes from erotic tomes
> By reading them all himself.
> Smite, Smoot, smite for Ut.,
> They're smuggling smut from Balt. to Butte!
> Strongest and sternest
> Of your s_x
> Scatter the scoundrels
> From Can. to Mex!

Smoot also fought back against those who argued that higher import duties would fail to help farmers. A study by University of Wisconsin economists John R. Commons, Benjamin H. Hibbard, and Selig Perlman found that many agricultural tariffs would not be effective in helping domestic producers. They concluded that the tariff would be fully effective on flax, olive oil, soybean oil, sugar, and wool; partially effective on buckwheat, butter, casein, milk and cream, sheep, lamb, and mutton, Swiss cheese, and high-protein wheat; and ineffective on barley, molasses, cheddar cheese, coconut oil, corn, cotton, jute, cottonseed oil, eggs, oats, rye, and other wheat. In terms of sugar, they calculated that the sugar duty cost the American public $289 million in higher prices in 1928, and the Smoot-Hawley duties would increase this to $384 million per year.[12]

Smoot rejected the report and these figures, saying that the "eminent economists" had made some "idiotic errors" and that "if they missed the mark half so widely as they missed the mark in sugar, every line of the tract is verbal rubbish." Smoot said that Congress was being asked to accept the advice of the economists "in a matter of which they have not the slightest practical knowledge" whereas "practical sugar men . . . have appeared before the Senate Finance Committee to tell of the absolute necessity of a higher rate on sugar. They have assured us that a higher rate is no threat to the consumer, and that it is no threat to the welfare of Cuba" (*Congressional Record*, January 10, 1930, 1368).

Although the coalition had modest success in reducing duties in the committee of the whole, Smoot and his allies won some key reversals late in the day. During its final stage of considering the bill in March, the Senate increased 75 duties (on imports valued $355 million) and decreased 31 duties (on $34 million of imports) from the version of the committee of the whole. As a result, insurgent Republicans began to lambast the bill. "The farmer has been betrayed by this bill," LaFollette thundered.

> The farmer's back has been made the springboard from which the industrial lobbyists have leaped to new and higher tariff rate levels for the benefit of the special industrial interests

[12] This report was reprinted in the *Congressional Record*, January 11, 1930, 1439–47.

they represent. The agricultural tariff granted the farmer, in many instances ineffective, carries with it the obligation to pay higher prices upon almost every article that is used upon the farm. (Congressional *Record*, March 24, 1930, 5977)

Branding it "the worst tariff bill" in the nation's history, LaFollette argued that the legislation would cost consumers a billion dollars in higher prices.

The Senate debate had been laborious and exhausting. The Senate had made 1,253 amendments to the House version, either technical or rate changes. The part of the floor debate that took place from September 1929 to February 1930 amounted to 527 hours and filled 2,638 pages of the *Congressional Record* at a printing cost of $131,000 (*New York Times*, March 30, 1930, 22). Numerous lengthy speeches were given, including Sen. Henry Ashurst's (D-AZ) fifteen pages on tomatoes and Sen. Gerald Nye's (R-ND) thirty-five pages on lumber.

At long last, the Senate completed its deliberations and passed the bill on March 24, 1930, ten months after its initial passage by the House. The final vote was 53–31; Republicans voted 46–5 in favor and Democrats voted 26–7 against. Because the Senate version included the export debenture and withheld flexible tariff authority from the president, many insurgents (including Borah) voted in favor of the bill, and only five Republicans opposed it.

As with the House bill, subsequent statistical analysis of the Senate's voting patterns concluded that partisan factors were dominant. Cupitt and Elliott (1994) examined several Senate roll call votes on specific amendments to the Smoot-Hawley tariff bill. They found that political party explains so much of the observed voting pattern

The Fellow That Is Always Left Out in the Rain
—Evans in the Columbus "Dispatch."

Source: *Columbus Dispatch*. Reprinted with permission from the *Columbus Dispatch*.

that there is little evidence of any influence of economic interests on these votes. Of course, a strictly partisan voting pattern is not inconsistent with economic interests playing an important role in shaping the tariff legislation. Because both political parties were large vote-trading entities with different constituencies, a partisan final vote does not necessarily reveal the role of specific economic interests. Irwin and Kroszner (1996) examined commodity-specific Senate votes using an empirical method to identify logrolling or vote-trading and found that the economic interests of various constituencies were crucial. Thus, the party-line vote on the final passage of the bill obscured a variety of special factors that shaped the structure of import duties in the final bill. Another question is what political and economic factors gave rise to the structure of tariff rates across different industries. Here, one statistical study obtained results that are "less clear cut as to which factors determined the ability [of producer groups] to influence policy" (Hayford and Pasurka 1992, 42).

Table 1.2 shows the import duties as the bill went through various versions. The average tariff rate in Schedule 7, the agricultural duties, rose from 22 percent in the existing tariff to 33 percent in the House bill to nearly 36 percent in the Senate version. This allowed members of Congress to claim that they had succeeded in delivering tariff equality to help farmers. However, other schedules, particularly earthenware and glassware schedules, were also increased significantly. This provided ammunition for the opponents to complain that manufacturers were benefiting from a tariff revision that was supposed to be mainly helping farmers.

The House-Senate Conference

Despite the Old Guard's success in finally getting the tariff bill through the Senate, the ultimate fate of the legislation was still in doubt. The differences between the House and Senate versions, particularly in terms of the

TABLE 1.2.
Proposed Tariff Duties at Various Stages of Congressional Consideration of the Smoot-Hawley Tariff

Product category	Act of 1913	Act of 1922	House Bill	Senate Finance Committee	Senate Committee of the Whole	Final Senate Bill
1. Chemicals, oils, paint	16.09	28.92	31.82	29.37	30.32	30.95
2. Earthenware & glassware	31.67	45.52	54.87	53.61	48.12	53.09
3. Metals	14.32	33.71	36.34	29.45	32.37	32.35
4. Wood	6.07	15.84	25.34	15.65	15.57	15.65
5. Sugar, molasses	39.23	67.85	92.36	84.75	68.17	77.15
6. Tobacco	60.66	63.09	66.96	63.09	63.09	63.09
7. Agricultural products	9.84	22.37	33.35	32.40	35.84	35.95
8. Alcoholic beverages	25.54	36.48	47.44	47.44	47.44	47.44
9. Cotton	30.53	40.27	43.19	43.19	37.64	40.59
10. Flax, hemp, jute	10.06	18.16	19.03	19.36	19.50	18.95
11. Wool	20.86	49.54	58.09	56.87	57.12	57.38
12. Silk	46.36	56.56	60.17	62.44	58.03	58.03
13. Rayon	34.34	52.68	53.42	53.78	53.64	49.14
14. Papers and books	21.67	24.51	26.14	26.13	25.63	25.91
15. Sundries	16.25	20.99	28.57	26.52	20.92	19.98
Average on comparable goods	21.08	34.61	43.15	40.54	37.84	39.98

Source: "Comparison of Rates of Duty in Pending Tariff Bill of 1929," Senate Document No. 119, 71st Congress, 2d Session, Washington, DC: GPO, 1930.

export debenture and the flexible tariff provision, were so wide that many believed that the bill would die in the conference committee. The House version had no export debenture and retained the flexible tariff provision, while the Senate had an export debenture and a modified flexible tariff provision that allowed Congress, not the president, to alter import duties after a Tariff Commission report. The president wanted to eliminate the export debenture and insisted upon a flexible tariff provision that gave the executive the power to change rates. If the Senate did not bow to the House and the president's demands, the conference would be deadlocked. And yet, the Senate voted to bind its conferees to maintain the export debenture and the modified flexible tariff provision. The prospect of a stalemate was quite real.

In April 1930, the House and Senate conference committee met to resolve the differences between the two versions of the bill. On the tariff rates, the two sides could compromise by splitting the difference or horse-trading across commodities. In general, the conference committee generally raised the tariff rates from the Senate version and put them closer to those in the original House version. In the end, out of the 3,293 dutiable items in the expanded tariff code, the final bill made 887 increases, 235 decreases, and left 2,171 duties untouched from the 1922 tariff. Of the 235 decreases, 75 minor goods were transferred to the duty-free list.

The stumbling blocks were the export debenture and flexible tariff provision. The House conferees refused to back down and rejected the Senate position, but the Senate conferees were bound by instructions not to recede from its version. In mid-May, the *New York Times* reported, "everything indicates that an awkward deadlock exists, with possibilities that it will continue for a protracted period and perhaps endanger the ultimate passage of the measure" (May 14, 1930, 6). Even Smoot was said to be "pessimistic" about the bill's fate.

The standoff promised to continue indefinitely until Smoot finally decided to ask the Senate to release the conferees from their obligations on the debenture and the flexible tariff. On May 18, the Old Guard won a crucial victory when the Senate narrowly voted to compromise on those provisions. In the case of dropping the export debenture, the final vote was 42–41. In the case of strengthening the flexible tariff provision, the vote was a 42–42 tie that was broken by the vice president. Without this retreat, the bill might very well have died from lack of House and Senate agreement. By bowing to the House demands, the Senate cleared the way for the bill's ultimate passage, but in so doing also alienated the insurgents, who had fought strenuously to keep the debenture in the bill.

The bill was not quite out of the woods yet. Through most of the legislative process, President Hoover had been largely silent. Apparently, he was not concerned about the height or structure of the tariff rates because he believed that the flexible tariff authority could be used to adjust the rates after the bill was passed. Now he threatened to veto the bill unless it included a stronger flexible tariff provision. The threat worked and the conference agreed to the president's demands. As Hoover (1952, 295–96) recalled:

> I learned on May 24 that the conferees had overridden Senator Smoot and Congressman Hawley and had watered the flexible provision down to about nothing. I wrote out the

provision I wanted. I sent word that unless my
formula was adopted, the bill would be vetoed.
The result was a complete victory for the flexible tariff in the conference report.

After wrangling over some remaining details, the
House and Senate conferees finally settled on a unified
bill. On June 13, 1930, the Senate passed the conference
bill by just two votes, 44–42. Republicans voted 39–11
in favor and Democrats voted 30–5 against (as did one
senator from the Farmer Labor Party). The close margin
reflected the loss of support from insurgent Republicans
who were dismayed that the conference bill stripped out
the export debenture and pushed industrial rates higher
than those passed by the Senate. Borah and other insurgents who had voted for the Senate bill because it included the debenture now voted against the conference
bill because they felt it betrayed agriculture. Although the
insurgents got eleven of fifty Republicans to vote against
the final bill, they were bitter about the outcome. Sen.
George Norris (R-NE) stated:

> From whatever standpoint we view the bill
> now before us I do not believe it can be de-
> fended. It represents protection run perfectly
> mad. It is conceived and written in the interest
> of victorious business organizations who are
> using their power, which they obtained by the
> practice, in my judgment, of many unfair and
> deceitful means, to put through the Congress
> one of the most selfish and indefensible tariff
> measures that has every been considered by the
> American people. In my judgment, those who

> are behind it will see that they have used their
> own power to bring about their own destruc-
> tion, because, after all, in the long run . . . a
> tariff bill which builds up a part of our people
> to the damage and injury of other parts of our
> people will bring its own ruin. (*Congressional
> Record*, June 12, 1930, 10546)

However, the votes of five Democrats were critical to the
Senate passage, and specific commodities convinced these
Democrats to support the measure: sugar in Louisiana,
wool in Wyoming, and fruit in Florida.

In the House, the final vote was an anticlimax, given the
Republican leadership's strong control over the party's
rank and file. The day after the Senate vote, the House
passed the conference bill in a party-line vote of 222–
153.[13] The debate before the final vote repeated many of
the arguments that had been voiced in previous months.
In urging its passage, Hawley predicted:

> [I]f this bill is enacted into law . . . we will have
> a renewed era of prosperity such as followed
> the enactment of every Republican tariff bill, in
> which all of the people of the United States in
> every occupation, every industry, and every em-
> ployment will share as they have always shared,
> which will increase our wealth, our employ-
> ment, our comfort, the means of supplying our
> necessities, that will promote our trade abroad,
> and keep the name of the United States still
> before the world as the premier nation of solid

---

[13] Republicans voted 208–20 in favor, while Democrats voted 132–14 against
(along with one representative from the Farmer Labor party).

THIS LITTLE PIG WENT TO MARKET!"
By Talburt, in the *Telegram* (New York)

Source: *New York World Telegram*

finance, fairness, and justice to all the people, and one which for all time intends to provide for its own. (*Congressional Record*, June 14, 1930, 10760)

Similarly, Rep. Frank Crowther (R-NY) predicted:

[O]nce this bill becomes a law, business confidence will be immediately restored. We shall gradually work out of the temporary slump we have been in for the last few months, and once more prosperity will reign supreme. Foreign reprisals will vanish into thin air and we shall continue to raise the standard of American labor and American wages. We shall dissipate the dark clouds of your gloomy prophesy with the rising sunshine of continued prosperity. (June 14, 1930, 10788–89)

Opponents attacked the final result with heated rhetoric. Sen. John Blaine (R-WI) criticized the bill as a "betrayal" of agriculture, saying: "The American farmer is not going to be fooled . . . he is going to know that fictitious tariff rates have been placed upon his products, rates from which he will receive no benefit and from which he cannot expect any benefit, while, on the other hand, rates on industrial commodities, which he must buy for use upon his farm in order to produce, have been raised to excessive and extortionate heights (*Congressional Record*, June 10, 1930, 10390). Sen. John Garner (D-TX) believed the bill

violates every precept of common sense, justice, and sound economics. Under the guise of protecting the products of agriculture, the Republican majority in both Houses has inflicted upon the country industrial rates that are indefensible; rates that can only serve to add to the burden the farmers and consumers have carried for years; rates that will tend to reduce, and in fact eliminate, the foreign markets for many of our products, both industrial and agricultural. (*Congressional Record*, June 14, 1930, 10761–62)

Garner continued:

Every attempt to give agriculture the advantage of equal protection has been defeated. Every effort to lower industrial rates to a point of parity with agricultural rates has met with the opposition of that small coterie of Republican leaders who have controlled the destinies of this bill. Those leaders raised a smoke screen under cover of which they manipulated the industrial rates to the highest point in the history of tariff making. They endeavored to camouflage this action by increasing rates on agricultural products of which a surplus is produced and upon which any tariff is inoperative. They flatly refused to accept the export debenture which would have made the tariff operative upon these surplus products of agriculture, and yet they have the audacity to refer to this bill as a measure designed for the relief of agriculture. (10762)

Finally, he concluded:

Bringing Home the Bacon
—Doyle in the Philadelphia "Record."

Source: *Philadelphia Record*

The Hawley-Smoot tariff is not the result of the application of economic facts derived from research and investigation. It is not the result of the application of scientific deduction or findings. It is the result of political subserviency to a small but powerful group, financially able to maintain in Washington a large and efficient corps of lobbyists and to control to a great extent the financial affairs as well as the policies of the Republican party. It is generally conceded that the lobbyists wrote and put over the Hawley-Smoot bill. Certainly there was no public demand for the indefensible rates contained in this measure. On the other hand, there was a widespread and vigorous demand that the rates either be reduced to place agriculture upon parity with industry or the bill defeated. (10764)

HOOVER'S DECISION

With Congress having passed the tariff, attention turned to the White House, where the bill went for President Hoover's signature. As noted earlier, the president was criticized at the time, and has been criticized by historians since, for his failure to provide more guidance to Congress regarding the duties written into the tariff bill. As the *Financial Chronicle* noted:

One of the most serious criticism[s] of Mr. Hoover is the prolonged tariff debate, which has been called out by his refusal to make known his views regarding rate revision, or his opinion of the seriousness of the protests against the tariff which have literally poured in upon him. There is little question that, if he had asserted himself, the country would have had a very different tariff from the one that has just been enacted. . . . It is difficult to believe . . . that Mr. Hoover finds in the tariff act much of which he can be proud but might not some

of the injustices, the excesses, and the palpable
unwisdom of the measure have been eliminated
if Mr. Hoover had firmly declared his opposition to them? (June 21, 1930, 4303)

Sen. Kenneth McKellar (D-TN) charged that Hoover
was responsible for "the muddled condition of the present tariff bill" because for sixteen months he "stood by in
silence, without the vision, leadership or courage" to demand that Congress restrict itself to a "limited" revision
of the tariff. Instead, the Republicans "proceeded calmly
to disregard the President's recommendation for limited
changes only in this measure and proceeded to revise the
entire tariff from top to bottom and to give us the highest
rates ever known" (*New York Times*, May 19, 1930, 4).[14]

The White House was inundated with letters and
telegrams urging the president to sign or veto the bill.
Hoover (1952, 296) later wrote that he was "deluged
with a mass of recommendations as to approval or veto
from representatives of a diversity of interests." Small and
medium-sized manufacturers supported the legislation, if
not for the actual benefits that they would receive then
at least for finally resolving uncertainty about Congress's
decision. Larger manufacturers, such as the automobile
industry, worried about foreign retaliation against American exports. The American Farm Bureau Federation, the
Farmers' Union, and the National Grange all endorsed

---

[14] Subsequent historians have also been very hard on Hoover for his failure
to show leadership earlier in the tariff-making process. "When the high-tariff
wolves took charge of the bill and began writing outrageous new duties into it,
he said nothing to rebuke them," historian Allan Nevins wrote. "His handling
of the whole situation showed an astonishing clumsiness" (Leuchtenburg 2009,
91). See also Snyder (1973).

President Herbert Hoover. Source: Library of Congress.

the measure, but other agricultural representatives were skeptical that it would help farmers very much. Organized labor was officially neutral, although individual unions took different positions depending upon how their industry was affected by imports or dependent on exports.[15]

Apart from interest groups, the public reaction to the Smoot-Hawley bill was largely negative. The president's correspondence secretary informed him that "there has seldom been in this country such a rising tide of protest as has been aroused by the tariff bill" (Leuchtenburg 2009, 92). Opposition to the bill was much more vocal than it had been with previous tariff acts, either because the economic rationale for the higher tariff was so weak, or because the public was more sensitive to the blatant role played by special interest politics and logrolling votes in Congress. The spectacle of the Senate voting multiple times on tariffs for the same goods, with the outcome shifting depending upon which coalition had the upper hand or which votes were traded among which senators, tarnished the body's image. It undermined any public confidence that the legislature could set tariffs free from political influence.

Of course, the public's view of the Smoot-Hawley tariff is difficult to measure because opinion polls were not routinely taken until the mid-1930s. However, a survey of 343 newspaper editors in forty-three states revealed that a vast majority did not consider it to be in the nation's best interest (Scroggs 1930). Opposition to the bill came from every region of the country. Nearly every Democratic

---

[15] In 1929, the president of the American Federation of Labor reaffirmed that the organization had "never committed itself to the support of a protective tariff or free trade. We have avoided most scrupulously and carefully that controversial field" (Leiter 1961, 56).

newspaper opposed the tariff bill, but so did 77 percent of independent papers as well as 45 percent of Republican newspapers. Three-fourths of the papers said that the tariff would not help farmers, would reduce foreign trade, and would have adverse effects on the economy (table 1.3). Among the papers that opposed the tariff, the opposition was strong and unequivocal; among the papers that supported the tariff, the support was tepid and even apologetic. Newspaper editorials charged that industrial lobbyists had written and paid for the bill. An independent Staten Island paper said the Smoot-Hawley tariff perpetuates "a vicious circle of local selfishness, which precludes any sane or intelligent treatment of the tariff question on a national scale," while a Republican newspaper in Jamestown, New York, called it a "hodge-podge of political expedience" (Scroggs 1930, 12).

Supporters of the bill dismissed the newspaper critics. Rep. Frank Crowther (R-NY) argued that "demagoguery and untruth, scandalous untruth, have been rampant ever since this bill passed the House of Representatives. Ever since that date editors, newspapermen, columnists, magazine writers, Democrats, and internationalists have all tumbled over themselves in their anxiety to see how much tirade and abuse they could heap upon this bill" (*Congressional Record*, June 14, 1930, 10787). The Republicans continued to argue that it would strengthen the economy and give producers an advantage in the domestic market.

In early May 1930, a group of American economists released a statement calling the higher tariffs "a mistake" and urging Congress to defeat the measure or the president to veto it. The widely publicized statement, signed by 1,028 economists from 179 colleges and universities,

TABLE 1.3.
Survey of Newspaper Editors: Views on the Tariff

	Yes	No	Undecided
	(percentage responses)		
Is the Smoot-Hawley bill in the best interests of the American people?	25	69	6
Will farmers in general benefit from the Smoot-Hawley bill?	26	74	—
Will U.S. foreign trade fall off if the tariff bill becomes law?	78	22	—
Has the long discussion of the bill in Congress had an adverse effect on American business and prosperity?	77	23	—

Source: Scroggs (1930).

was prominently reported on the front page of the *New York Times* on May 5, 1930, reprinted in the *Congressional Record*, and widely commented upon in the press. (The statement is reproduced in the appendix.) The *Financial Chronicle* called it "a document without parallel in American history. Never before has a great body of scholarly and expert opinion voluntarily arranged itself en masse in opposition to a pending piece of national legislation" (May 10, 1930, 3247).

The economists argued that American manufacturers did not need greater tariff protection: "Already our factories supply our people with over 96 percent of the manufactured goods which they consume, and our producers look to foreign markets to absorb the increasing output of their machines. Further barriers to trade will serve them not well, but ill." Greater protection would increase consumer prices, leading to greater profits for efficient, low-cost firms and encouraging greater production by inefficient, high-cost firms. The majority of workers who did not produce goods that could be protected by tariffs would lose, the economists contended, and farmers would be doubly hit, first in paying a higher price for the manufactured goods that they consume and then in facing greater obstacles to exporting abroad. Indeed, exports would suffer because "countries cannot permanently buy from us unless they are permitted to sell to us, and the more we restrict importation of goods from them by means of even higher tariffs, the more we reduce the possibility of exporting to them." Finally, higher tariffs would "inevitably inject . . . bitterness" into international economic relations and "plainly invite other nations to compete with us in raising further barriers to trade" (*Congressional Record*, May 5, 1930, 8327–30).

When asked his view of the economists' statement, Willis Hawley said: "My opinion of it cannot be printed" (*Financial Chronicle*, May 10, 1930, 3289). Other supporters of the bill rejected the economists' advice. Rep. David O'Connell (R-NY) said: "I have no patience with the economists that are consistently raising flimsy objections to this legislation" (*Congressional Record*, May 5, 1930, 8383). Sen. Samuel Shortridge (R-CA) was similarly dismissive: "I am not overawed and I am not at all disturbed by the proclamation of the college professors who never earned a dollar by the sweat of their brow by honest labor—theorists, dreamers—I am not overawed or disturbed by their pronunciamentos, nor am I disturbed at all by the poll of newspapers, whether they be metropolitan journals or village publications" (*Congressional Record*, May 10, 1930, 9133). Sen. Henry Hatfield (R-WV) stated: "Cloistered in colleges as they are, hidden behind a mass of statistics, these men have no opportunity to view the practical side of life in matters pertaining to our industrial welfare as a nation." He scorned these "intellectual free traders, who seem to be more concerned with the prosperity of foreigners than they are with the well-being of our own American people" (*Congressional Record*, May 28, 1930, 9704).[16]

Leading commentators, financiers, industrialists, and other advisors also told Hoover to reject the tariff bill. The respected journalist Walter Lippmann criticized it as "a wretched and mischievous product of stupidity and greed" (Steel 1980, 288). Executives of banks and financial institutions reminded Hoover that the United States became a creditor nation after World War I and that high tariffs, by diminishing the ability of other countries to earn the dollars needed to pay their war debts, could potentially destabilize the international financial system. Thomas Lamont of J.P. Morgan, an advisor to Hoover, recalled: "I almost went down on my knees to beg Her-

---

[16]Members of Congress had long been skeptical of academic economists for their support for freer trade. As Smoot once said: "Powerful forces are at work to break down American protection. They lurk in the international economic conferences held in Europe, in American schools of economics, and in the cloistered halls of theoretical universities. No greater calamity could come to the United States and our people than blind obedience to these forces" (*Congressional Record*, September 12, 1929, 3550).

bert Hoover to veto the asinine Hawley-Smoot Tariff. That Act intensified nationalism all over the world" (Burner 1979, 298). Henry Ford reportedly spent time with Hoover and told him that Smoot-Hawley was "an economic stupidity" (Klingaman 1989, 334). Secretary of State Henry Stimson is said to have "fought like mad" for two days in an attempt to persuade Hoover to veto the measure (Morison 1960, 312).

It is difficult to know whether Hoover had any serious reservations about signing the bill.[17] Presidential historian Richard Norton Smith (1984, 114) relates the following pathetic story:

> A friendly industrialist cast aside the president's feeble arguments that the bill had been rendered less objectionable than it might have been. What did it matter that Hoover found the bill marginally acceptable when the country found it pernicious? And what of the president's own function as a leader and educator of men? Hoover stopped his doodling. In a voice that barely carried beyond his desk, he justified his actions while apologizing for them. "I'm

[17] Hoover is often quoted as saying that the bill was "vicious, extortionate, and obnoxious." Unfortunately, the source for this story is not credible: the 1931 gossip book *Washington Merry-Go-Round* by Washington journalists Drew Pearson and Robert Allen, who were known for making many unsubstantiated allegations. They wrote: "The Old Guard high-tariff gang cowed [Hoover] into signing the Smoot-Hawley Tariff Act which in a thousand ways violated every view he had ever held on the tariff and which, up to a few hours before he furtively announced his approval, he had described to his friends as vicious, extortionate and obnoxious" (65–66). Regardless of whether he ever actually described the bill in those terms, the bill clearly did not violate "every view" he had on the tariff because he repeatedly endorsed protective tariffs throughout his career.

afraid you'll have to give me up," he remarked to his erstwhile admirer. "I can never be the sort of man you want me to be."

Despite all the pleas, there was no way that the president could have vetoed the bill at this late date, especially once Congress agreed to his demands on the flexible tariff and export debenture. Hoover never seemed to care about the tariff rates themselves. His concern was to keep the flexible tariff provision in and get the export debenture out of the bill. Given that a Republican Congress had delivered tariff legislation that a Republican president had requested, and that the conference committee adopted the president's version of the flexible tariff provision, it would have been almost impossible for him to justify vetoing the bill.[18]

Yet, perhaps because of all the public criticism, there seemed to be some lingering uncertainty about whether the president would sign the bill. The uncertainty was resolved late Sunday night, June 14, 1930, when the White House announced that he would approve it. The next day, share prices on the New York Stock Ex-

[18] As Merrill (1990, 332) points out: "Hoover has been subjected to scathing criticism for his failure to veto the Smoot-Hawley bill. Approval of the bill was not the president's major mistake. It was his failure to assume leadership of the party in the spring and summer of 1929. By remaining silent during 1929 and the early months of 1930, except on the flexible tariff and debenture provision, Hoover, in effect, approved the bill in advance. It was too late to veto the bill in June 1930. It would have been a repudiation of all his congressional supporters, and abject surrender to the Democrats and Insurgents, a sorry reward to those stalwarts, such as Smoot, who had labored prodigiously to include the flexible provision and eliminate the debenture in response to presidential wishes. The 1,028 economists who petitioned Hoover to veto the bill should have exerted their substantial pressure one year earlier." Koyama (2009) stresses Hoover's interest in the flexible tariff provision as the main reason he signed the bill.

change dropped 1.16 percent. As one financial publication reported:

> President Hoover, regarding whose intentions with respect to the Tariff Bill there had been expressions of doubt, took pains to let it be known on Sunday night . . . that he would sign the Bill. Instead of this providing an aid to the markets, however, it acted in the reverse manner, the financial community looking upon the bill with disfavor because it raised the tariff barriers still higher. The Stock Exchange now became actually swamped with selling orders. . . . The commodity markets were equally depressed and cotton, grain, and a whole host of other articles reached new low figures for the year. (*The Annalist*, June 20, 1930, 10)[19]

The next day the White House released a statement by the president detailing his reasons for approving the legislation. As Hoover (1976, 232–33) described the bill:

> It contains many compromises between sectional interests and between different industries. No tariff bill has ever been enacted or ever will be enacted under the present system

[19] The *New York Times* added: "Coming on the heels of President Hoover's announcement that he would sign the new tariff bill, a torrent of liquidation swept over the stock market yesterday with devastating force, driving prices to the lowest levels of the year. . . . There was a feeling of discouragement that extended to all of the speculative markets. Everywhere the disposition was to lay the blame at the doors of Congress. Loud lamentations against the tariff bill were heard throughout the financial district" (June 17, 1930, 1).

that will be perfect. A large portion of the items are always adjusted with good judgment, but it is bound to contain some inequalities and inequitable compromises. There are items upon which duties will prove too high and others upon which duties will prove to be too low. Certainly no President, with his other duties, can pretend to make that exhaustive determination of the complex facts which surround each of those 3,300 items, and which has required the attention of hundreds of men in Congress for nearly a year and a third. That responsibility must rest upon the Congress in a legislative rate revision.

For Hoover, the flexible tariff provision was the main reason to sign the bill: "I believe that the flexible provisions can within reasonable time remedy inequalities; that this provision is a progressive advance and gives great hope of taking the tariff away from politics, lobbying, and logrolling."

But Hoover was anxious also to dispose of the whole matter: "It is urgent that the uncertainties in the business world which have been added to by the long-extended debate of the measure should be ended. . . . As I have said, I do not assume the rate structure in this or any other tariff bill is perfect, but I am convinced that the disposal of the whole question is urgent. . . . Nothing would so retard business recovery as continued agitation over the tariff." Now, he concluded, "the country should be freed from further general revision for many years to come. Congressional revisions are not only disturbing to business but with all their necessary collateral surroundings in lobbies, log rolling, and the activities of group interests, are disturbing to public confidence."

Hoover signed the Tariff Act of 1930 on June 17, 1930 at 12:59 p.m. in a small White House ceremony. It took effect the next morning. Hoover never expressed regret about signing the bill and he continued to defend it, in later years and during the 1932 election campaign. Reflecting on these events many years later, however, Hoover (1952, 299) conceded that "raising the tariff from its sleep was a political liability despite the virtues of its reform."

The Smoot-Hawley Tariff in Perspective

The Smoot-Hawley tariff of 1930 has been popularly portrayed as an aberration, an atrocious piece of legislation that reflected special interest politics and logrolling run amok. Yet, in light of previous Republican policies, the Smoot-Hawley tariff was not completely out of the ordinary. Given the economic difficulties afflicting agriculture during the 1920s, it was not unusual for the Republicans to call for a revision of the tariff during the election campaign of 1928. The degree to which the Smoot-Hawley legislation increased import duties was also not unprecedented, as chapter 2 will discuss. And, of course, logrolling had always been a part of tariff legislation, even in the Democratic tariffs of 1894 and 1913, although it became much more blatant in 1930.

That said, it is easier to explain the political rationale behind the Fordney-McCumber tariff of 1922 than it is to explain the Smoot-Hawley tariff of 1930. After the 1920 election, political control shifted from the Democrats to the Republicans, who had a strong desire to reverse the existing low-tariff policy enacted by the Democrats. In addition, the economy was suffering from a severe recession brought about by erratic monetary adjustments after World War I. None of these factors was present at the start of the Smoot-Hawley revision. The Republicans had uninterrupted control of government during the 1920s. Work on the Smoot-Hawley tariff was begun when the economy was close to a business cycle peak—the unemployment rate was only about 3 percent in 1929—and the stock market crash and recession came after the House had passed the bill and while the Senate was considering it. The revision lacked any strong economic rationale, and most independent observers thought it was not only unnecessary but harmful.

The Smoot-Hawley tariff was unique on several dimensions. The legislation took much longer than any previous tariff legislation to move from the House hearings to final congressional passage—eighteen months, from January 1929 to June 1930. At almost two hundred pages, the Smoot-Hawley bill was also significantly longer and more complex than its predecessors. The bill specified tariff rates on almost 3,300 enumerated items, thus making it unwieldy, and difficult for Congress to manage.

The legislative ordeal was the source of immense frustration for members of both parties and those in the general public who cared about the measure. Day after day Congress found itself debating the appropriate import duty on items such as clothes pins, cordage, silk hats, glass rods, hempseed oil, paper board, and zinc-bearing ores, when it could have been working on other matters. Of the 257 Senate roll call votes taken between

September 10, 1929 and March 24, 1930, 228 concerned the tariff. The tortuous path and unsatisfactory outcome of the Smoot-Hawley legislation made members of Congress painfully aware of the inanities involved in revising customs duties. As Sen. Thaddeus Caraway (D-AR) noted:

> The trouble is the system. The instances are many where protection is accorded to those industries that least need it, while others, really deserving, are passed or else not given the protection to which they are entitled. Just look at the schedules in the bill now before the Senate. The rates in that bill bear no appreciable relation to imports, and very frequently they bear little, if any, relation to the earning capacity of the individuals or the corporations seeking higher duties. (*New York Times*, November 10, 1929, 21)

The problem was that each member of Congress looked out for the special producer interests in his or her particular district without considering the broader national interest, particularly those not represented in the legislative process. Sen. David Walsh (D-MA) stated as much: "The existing minuteness with respect to rates is partly an absurdity and partly a partisan fraud to cover up what the tariff really is—namely, a mass of private legislation" (*New York Times*, November 10, 1929, 11). For example, even though the ratio of imports to domestic consumption of white potatoes was 1.24 percent in 1927, Rep. Carroll Beedy (R-ME) defended the higher duty on imported potatoes:

> I am espousing no local issue. It is true that the tariff in many instances is a local issue. But the inadequately protected American potato is a nation-wide issue. (*Congressional Record*, May 16, 1929, 1424)

What subjected the Senate to public ridicule was the spectacle of the body holding multiple votes on the precise tariff rate to be imposed on a bewildering array of obscure imports. The Senate considered and reconsidered the tariff on various chemicals—tannic acid, calcium carbide, casein, lithium, beryllium caesium—and other products ranging from olive oil, cork insulation, straw hats, crude gypsum, crushed gypsum, dates, lard, cordage, pipe organs, mustard seed, buttons, umbrellas, beeswax, and broomcorn. And there were separate votes on carbonized wool noils, wool rags, wool yarn, wool waste, and so forth. Members of Congress spent an enormous amount of time debating innumerable commodities that most of them had little information about.

The lack of any particular economic rationale in setting the tariff rates was also disturbing. "Despite a pretense in the debates that there was some objective test of national welfare," economist Frank Fetter (1933, 418) noted, "the record of voting on individual items furnishes much evidence in support of the cynical proposition that sound protection was that which raised the prices of things produced by one's constituents, and unsound protection that which raised the prices of things made by someone's else constituents." The changes in the tariff rates bore little relationship to the old Republican objective of setting tariffs to equalize differences in the costs of production between domestic and foreign producers. Whereas the Tariff Commission purported to show that a 31 percent duty on imported canned tomatoes would "equalize" the cost of production, Congress set the duty at 50 percent. When the Commission found that a tariff on flaxseed of 56 cents per bushel would equalize costs, Congress set the tariff at 65 cents.[20] In fact, by the time of the Smoot-Hawley revision, Republicans effectively abandoned "differences in costs of production" criteria for "differences in conditions of competition," a vaguer and much more elastic guideline.

The final outcome satisfied very few of the interested parties and drew widespread criticism from the public. Even worse, the two major premises behind the tariff revision were flawed: that it could bring relief to farmers and that the flexible tariff provision could smooth out the iniquities in the tariff.

The Republicans started down the road of tariff revision on the pretense that it would help agriculture. Yet, as noted before, the key problems facing most farmers—low prices and high indebtedness—could not be ameliorated through import restrictions because most farmers did not face competition from imports. Most farmers produced goods that were exported, and they suffered from low prices on the world market, a problem that an import tariff would do nothing to change. In the end, most farmers were simply not in a position to receive many economic benefits from restricting imports through high tariffs. As Rep. John Garner (D-TX) pointed out:

[20] These examples and many more come from Bidwell (1930).

The contention of the supporters of this bill
that it is an agricultural measure is ridiculous.
With few exceptions the increases upon agricultural products are inoperative, and practically every increase upon the products of
manufactures is operative. . . . Every attempt
to give agriculture the advantage of equal protection has been defeated. (*Congressional Record*,
June 14, 1930, 10762)

Subsequent studies confirmed that the Smoot-Hawley
tariff actually reduced the effective rate of protection received by agricultural producers because the duties on
other goods were increased even more.[21]

In terms of the flexible tariff provision, Hoover was de-
luded by the hope that it could be used to reform the tariff code. Although Hoover may have wanted to do more
with the flexible tariff provision, past experience had
given little reason to expect significant changes. Although
the goal was to reduce excessive tariffs that crept into the
tariff code, the provision had not worked that way under
the Republicans in the 1920s. Very few tariff rates were
changed using the flexible tariff provision, partly because
each proposed change required a time-consuming investigation by the Tariff Commission. From 1922 to 1929,
the commission received more than 600 applications for
rate changes on 375 commodities, yet it only completed
47 investigations on 55 commodities (Kelley 1963, 18–

[21] Archibald, Feldman, Hayford, and Pasurka (2000) calculate how the structure of duties in the Smoot-Hawley act changed the effective rates of protection for a number of products and find that it generally lowered protection for
agriculture.

19). Over that period, the Tariff Commission issued 41 reports to the president recommending changes in duties and the president issued 37 proclamations that changed duties. Only five were reductions, and those on minor and obscure products: mill feed, bobwhite quail, paintbrush handles, phenol, and cresylic acid.[22] Despite Hoover's success in keeping the provision intact, it was hardly used in subsequent years.[23]

The political scientist E. E. Schattschneider, whose work on the Smoot-Hawley tariff was mentioned earlier, attributed the act not to party politics or an ideological attachment to protection, but to the absence of any force that would stop producer groups from demanding and receiving higher duties once the idea of a tariff revision had been broached. Yet because he focused almost exclusively on the public hearings, Schattschneider provided an incomplete—indeed, a very misleading—picture of the whole legislative process. It is certainly true that Congress received a very biased view of the range of economic interests affected by tariff legislation at committee hearings, where only a small number of producer interests tended to participate. But by choosing to focus

[22] Duties were increased in thirty-two cases, such as sixteen types of chemicals, wheat flour, butter, straw hats, print rollers, and pig iron, as well as on narrowly defined commodities such as taximeters, men's sewed straw hats, sodium nitrate, precipitated barium carbonate, and onions, often by the full 50 percent allowed.

[23] In the period from June 18, 1930, to November 30, 1933, the Tariff Commission initiated 105 investigations, 61 at the request of the Senate, 9 by order of the president, and 35 by application of interested parties. Only 57 investigations had been completed, resulting in the president's decision to decrease 26 rates of duty and increase 23 rates and 8 left unchanged (U.S. Tariff Commission 1933). The decreases were on such goods as edible gelatin, olive oil, feldspar, bent-wood furniture, wood flour, eggplant, pipe organs, and sheep-wool sponges.

Mr. Hoover: "Leave It to Willie"
—Spencer in the Omaha "World-Herald."

Source: *Omaha World Herald*. Reprinted with permission of the *Omaha World Herald*.

on the committee hearings and not the debates on the House and Senate floor, Schattschneider did not mention that most Democrats in both chambers and Republican agricultural interests in the Senate strongly opposed the bill. The battle over the bill was contentious and difficult, and Congress did not simply accede to whatever private interests demanded.

CONCLUSION

One of the ironies of the Smoot-Hawley tariff is that it did not originate primarily as a result of interest group pressure. By and large, the nation's manufacturers were not clamoring for higher duties in 1928 or 1929, and the nation's farmers, recognizing that higher import duties would have a limited effect on domestic prices, wanted some form of subsidy to relieve their financial woes. Refusing to consider subsidies, Republican politicians offered up a tariff in the hopes that it would placate farm interests and demonstrate that they were doing something to help agriculture. Once the door to a tariff change was opened, some groups—particularly small and medium-sized manufacturers—were only too happy to take up the offer and seek higher duties on imports for themselves. The process spun out of control and, as a result, the Smoot-Hawley tariff will forever be associated with logrolling, special interest politics, and inability of members of Congress to think beyond their own district. The episode illustrates that politicians are just as guilty as interest groups when it comes to using economic legislation to their benefit. The politicians were more interested in the appearance rather than the reality of helping farmers cope with low prices and high indebtedness.

In terms of the political strategy, the Smoot-Hawley tariff represented a huge miscalculation by progressive Republican insurgents. William Borah had pressed president-elect Hoover for a special session of Congress to address the farm situation through a tariff revision. The progressives believed that Congress would alter import duties in a way that would benefit their agrarian constituents and possibly include an export debenture, despite the Republican leadership's failure to do either in the past. The insurgents underestimated the resistance to reducing duties on manufactured goods and overestimated how much others would agree to their demands. They came to regret the consequences.

Chapter 2
Economic Consequences

During the summer of 1929, as the Senate began considering the House bill, the United States reached a business cycle peak. Over the next four years, the nation would experience an unrelenting economic contraction known as the Great Depression. Although the economic decline began nearly a year before the new tariff took effect in June 1930, many have sought to blame the Smoot-Hawley tariff for turning a recession into a full-blown depression.

Before we can examine this controversial claim, we have to resolve an even more basic dispute about how much the legislation increased tariffs and reduced imports. The Smoot-Hawley tariff is commonly thought to have raised U.S. import duties to absurdly high levels. For example, Gottfried Haberler (1976) suggested that the act pushed tariffs to "skyscraper" heights. Others have said that such statements are an exaggeration. Alfred Eckes (1995) contends that Smoot-Hawley was not a mountain but a "molehill." To assess the economic effects of the tariff, the first step is to determine how much the legislation raised import duties.

As the House was preparing to vote on the final passage of the bill, Willis Hawley reported calculations the Tariff Commission made regarding the duties in the final bill (table 2.1, columns 1 and 3). It showed that if the rates of duty in the final 1930 legislation had been applied to actual imports in 1928, it would have pushed the average tariff on dutiable imports from 38.75 percent to 41.14 percent, an increase of about 6 percent (2.4 percentage points).[1] However, this calculation, never published by the Tariff Commission, is inconsistent with a calculation that the Tariff Commission published in March 1930, presented in table 1.3. The March 1930 calculation suggested that the House bill would increase import duties by 25 percent and the Senate bill by 16 percent. Since the conference committee adopted rates closer to those in the House bill, it seems that the final calculation should have been an increase closer to 20 percent.

Two factors are responsible for the small percent increase presented by Hawley. First, unlike the Tariff Commission's March 1930 calculation, the first column in table 2.1 calculates the tariff without including goods that were duty-free under the 1922 act but that became dutiable under the 1930 act. By excluding those goods, Hawley increased the estimate of the average tariff under the 1922 rates; by including those goods, the average tariff under 1922 rates falls from 38.75 percent to 34.6

[1] This is a static calculation that assumes imports remain fixed at their 1928 amounts.

TABLE 2.1.

The Smoot-Hawley Tariff by Tariff Classification Schedule

Tariff schedule	Act of 1922 (1)	Act of 1922 Revised (2)	Act of 1930 (3)
	(percentage)		
1. Chemicals, oils, paint	29.72	28.92	36.09
2. Earthenware & glassware	48.33	45.52	53.73
3. Metals and manufactures of	35.19	33.71	35.08
4. Wood and manufactures of	24.78	15.84	11.73
5. Sugar, molasses, and manufactures of	67.85	67.85	77.21
6. Tobacco and manufactures of	63.09	63.09	64.78
7. Agricultural products and provisions	22.71	21.25	35.07
8. Spirits, wines, and other beverages	38.83	36.48	47.44
9. Manufactures of cotton	40.27	40.27	46.42
10. Flax, hemp, jute, and manufactures of	18.16	18.16	19.14
11. Wool and manufactures of	49.54	49.54	59.83
12. Manufactures of silk	56.56	56.56	59.13
13. Manufactures of rayon	57.75	52.68	53.62
14. Papers and books	25.02	24.51	26.06
15. Sundries	37.76	25.86	28.45
Total (Comparable Goods)	38.75	35.65	41.14

Source: Columns 1 and 3 from *Congressional Record*, June 14, 1930, 10748. Column 2 based on adjustments noted in text.

Note: Duties computed using the 1928 value and volume of imports.

percent, making the change brought about by the Smoot-Hawley bill larger. Second, in the June 1930 calculation that Hawley presented, the average tariff in the sundries schedule drops about nine percentage points. This drop did not actually occur. Rather, the anomaly arose because of a technical difference in calculating the average tariff under the 1922 duties and the 1930 duties. When the comparable calculation is made, the average tariff for the sundry schedule should be 25.86 percent under the 1922 rates, not the 37.76 percent reported by Hawley.[2]

These two corrections, presented in column 2 of table 2.1, reduce the average tariff under the 1922 rates to 35.65 percent, instead of the 38.75 percent reported by Hawley. What is the implication of this change? If the average tariff on dutiable imports in 1928 was 35.65 percent using the rates in the 1922 act and 41.14 percent using the rates in the 1930 rates, the average increase is 15.4 percent (or 5.5 percentage points)—much larger than the 6 percent figure reported by Hawley.

The actual figures on the average tariff on dutiable imports, as measured by customs revenue as a share of dutiable imports, are consistent with this revision. The average tariff on dutiable imports rose from 38.4 percent in the first quarter of 1930 to 48.3 percent in the three months from August to October 1930, an increase of 25.7 percent (almost ten percentage points) in the average

---

[2] Smoot made reference to the anomaly in his remarks, noting that Sen. Frank Crowther (R-NY) called it an "oversight." Such a large drop was never contemplated; in the March 1930 Tariff Commission comparison, the average tariff on sundries went from 20.99 percent to 28.57 percent in the House bill and down to 19.98 percent in the Senate bill. The March 1930 Tariff Commission calculation put the average tariff on sundries at 20.99 percent under the 1922 duties, but the June 1930 calculation put it at 37.8 percent, once again because it excluded the duty-free imports that became dutiable under the 1930 law.

rate of duty.[3] For reasons that will be discussed shortly, the tariff probably would have risen 7.6 percent during this period anyway because import prices fell 13 percent between the first and third quarters of 1930.[4] Taking into account this rise in the tariff that would have happened without Smoot-Hawley, these data suggest that the Smoot-Hawley tariff increased the average tariff on dutiable imports by about 18 percent (6.4 percentage points). This was enough to move the average tariff from 38.4 percent to 45.4 percent.

Although there will inevitably be some uncertainty about how much the Smoot-Hawley tariff raised import duties, the best guess is that it probably raised the average tariff on dutiable imports by about 15–18 percent, an increase of about 6 percentage points. Of course, this is an average effect; because many of the duties in the tariff code were left unchanged, those that were changed increased much more than this figure suggests.

Historically, the Smoot-Hawley increase was not extreme. It was significantly less than the Fordney-McCumber tariff of 1922, which pushed up the average tariff rate by 64 percent (more than 13 percentage points) from the tariff enacted in 1913 by the Democrats. The Underwood-Simmons tariff of 1913 reduced rates by more than 30 percent (13 percentage points) from its previous level.

[3] The second quarter of 1930 is not representative because it was affected by a large surge of imports seeking to enter the country before the tariff was imposed, particularly May and June. This analysis also excludes the third quarter of 1930 because the month of July was affected by the tariff's imposition. These data are from the Department of Commerce's *Monthly Summary of Foreign Commerce*.

[4] The effect arises because lower import prices increase the ad valorem equivalent of the specific duties in the tariff code. The percentage change in import prices must be multiplied by -0.6 to estimate the impact on the average tariff (Irwin 1998a). In this case, $-0.127 \times -0.6 = 0.76$.

The McKinley tariff of 1890 increased tariffs on dutiable imports by about 10 percent (four percentage points).

Nevertheless, the Smoot-Hawley duties provoked controversy in part because they marked a further addition that came on top of the already high Fordney-McCumber duties. Furthermore, the tariff did not simply jump in 1930 and then stop. Figure 2.1 shows the average tariff on dutiable and total imports during this period. The average tariff on dutiable imports increased in 1930, but then rose further in 1931 and again in 1932, when it peaked at 59.1 percent, the second highest recorded value in U.S. history.[5] This is one reason for the perception that tariffs were lifted to "skyscraper" heights during this period.

The legislated increase in import duties in 1930 was only partly responsible for the higher tariff during this period. Severe deflation in import prices also contributed to the rise of the average tariff on dutiable imports in 1931 and 1932. How did this happen? There are two types of duties applied to imports: ad valorem duties (a percentage of the good's value, such as 15 percent) and specific duties (a fixed dollar amount, such as 42 cents per bushel).[6] If

---

[5] The average tariff on dutiable imports reached 61.7 percent in 1830, shortly after the enactment of the Tariff of Abominations in 1828. Of course, the average tariff on total imports was much lower in 1932 (at 19.6 percent) than in 1830 (at 57.3 percent) because many imports were duty-free in 1932, whereas in 1830, revenue considerations required that virtually all imports be taxed.

[6] An example of an ad valorem tariff from the Tariff Act of 1930 is from Paragraph 208(f) of Schedule 2 (Earths, Earthenware, and Glassware) which read: "Untrimmed phlogopite mica from which no rectangular piece exceeding two inches in length or one inch in width may be cut, 15 per centum ad valorem." An example of a specific duty is from paragraph 1105 of Schedule 11 (Wool and manufactures of): "Top waste, slubbing waste, roving waste, and ring waste, 37 cents per pound; garnetted waste, 26 cents per pound; noils, carbonized, 30 cents per pound; thread or yarn waste, 25 cents per pound, card or burr waste, carbonized, 23 cents per pound; not carbonized, 16 cents per pound; all other wool waste not specially provided for, 24 cents per pound."

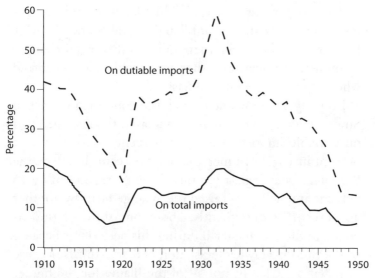

Figure 2.1. Average U.S. tariff on imports. Source: U.S. Department of Commerce (1976), series U211-212.

import prices fall, the ad valorem rate stays the same, but the value of a specific duty in terms of the percentage of the good's value increases. For example, if imports of shirts are charged $5 per unit and the average price is $20, the tax rate is 25 percent. If the price of shirts falls to $10 and the import duty remains at $5 per unit, the tariff rate, or ad valorem equivalent, has doubled from 25 percent to 50 percent.

At the time of Smoot-Hawley, about two-thirds of dutiable imports in the U.S. tariff code were subject to specific duties. Import prices plunged in the early 1930s, falling 18 percent in 1930, 22 percent in 1931, and another 22 percent in 1932. Because of falling prices, the average tariff on dutiable imports crept up to 53 percent in 1931 and to 59 percent in 1932.[7] This deflation-induced increase in the tariff was unrelated to the Smoot-Hawley legislation: it began in 1929 and was driven by changes in monetary policy, and therefore would have occurred whether or not the bill had passed.[8]

Looking at the whole period, the combined impact of Smoot-Hawley and deflation increased the average tariff on dutiable imports from 40.1 percent in 1929 to 59.1 percent in 1932—an increase of 47 percent. In effect, the Smoot-Hawley legislation raised the average tariff by 16 percent and deflation raised the average tariff by another 30 percent.[9] Consequently, about one-third of the increase in the average tariff during this period was because of the Smoot-Hawley legislation and two-thirds because of deflation. Clearly, not all of the blame for the higher tariff in the early 1930s can be placed on Senator Smoot and Congressman Hawley.

THE IMPACT ON IMPORTS

How much did the higher Smoot-Hawley tariff reduce imports? There are two reasons to expect that it had a modest effect on imports: its limited impact on the domestic prices of imported goods and its limited applicability to imports.

First, the impact on the price of dutiable imports was limited. A 16 percent increase in the tariff does not mean that the domestic price of imports increases by 16 percent. If the average tariff on dutiable imports rises from

---

[7] For an analysis of this phenomena, see Crucini (1994) and Irwin (1998a).

[8] Conversely, inflation in import prices account for much of the decline in tariffs between 1932 and 1950, as seen in figure 2.1; cf. Irwin 1998a.

[9] Import prices fell 50 percent from 1929 to 1932, so $-0.5 \times -0.6 = 0.3$.

38.4 percent to 45.4 percent, the domestic price of those imports would increase by just 5 percent. In other words, an imported good that costs $1 would, taking the tariff into account, sell for $1.38 before Smoot-Hawley and $1.45 after Smoot-Hawley—an increase of 5 percent.[10] Of course, as mentioned earlier, we have to keep in mind that this is an average effect: since many import duties did not change in the 1930 legislation, the prices of those goods subject to the higher duties would have increased much more. Still, overall, consumers would not have noticed a big change.

The other issue limiting the impact of the tariff was the fact that only a third of U.S. imports in 1929 were subject to import duties at all. High tariffs discouraged dutiable imports, but two-thirds of imports entered the United States free of duty even before the Smoot-Hawley duties took effect. These duty-free raw materials and consumer goods did not, by and large, compete with domestic producers. In 1929, the ten largest duty-free imports were, in terms of descending value, raw silk, coffee, rubber, copper, paper, petroleum, hides and skins, paper base stocks, furs, and tin. Thus, the higher duties under the Smoot-Hawley tariff fell on only a relatively small portion of total imports.

One way to assess the impact of the Smoot-Hawley tariff on imports is simply to look at monthly data on the value of imports. Figure 2.2 presents the value of dutiable and duty-free imports during this period and is quite revealing. In June 1930, imports surged into the

---

[10] To take an extreme example, if the rate of import duty doubled, from 1 percent to 2 percent, the domestic price would not double. The price effect is calculated as $(1+t_1) / (1+t_0) - 1$, where t_0 is the initial tariff and t_1 is the new tariff.

country, increasing dutiable imports by 26 percent from the previous month. This reflects the anticipation of new duties that would take effect when the fate of the Smoot-Hawley tariff was finally resolved. As we saw in chapter 1, in early May 1930 it was still unclear whether the House and Senate could reconcile their two versions of the bill, and whether Hoover would ultimately sign it. In mid-May, when the Senate agreed to drop the export debenture and give the president flexible tariff authority, the bill's prospects improved considerably. As a result, importers brought a flood of goods into U.S. ports, hoping that the goods could clear customs before the higher duties in the new tariff took effect. There were numerous press reports of ships racing to reach New York before the bill became law.

The sharp drop in dutiable imports after June 1930 is also clearly evident in the figure. Excluding the temporary June import surge, the value of dutiable imports fell 34 percent between the three months prior to the tariff's imposition (March–May 1930) and three months following its imposition (July–September 1930). The value of duty-free imports fell 21 percent over the same period. If we consider duty-free imports as a control group that indicates how much dutiable imports would have fallen without any tariff change, the Smoot-Hawley act apparently reduced the value of dutiable imports by about 13 percent—a reduction of $190 million off the 1929 value of imports. Since dutiable imports comprised one-third of total imports, we can suppose that the value of total imports fell about 4.4 percent as a result of the Smoot-Hawley tariff. Other estimates of the decline in dutiable imports are very similar, if somewhat higher, at about

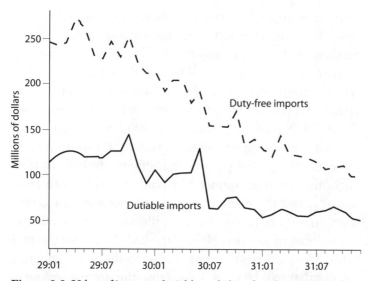

Figure 2.2. Value of imports, dutiable and-duty free, by month, 1929–1931. Source: Monthly Summary of Foreign Commerce, December 1930 and December 1931 issues.

16–17 percent.[11] From these estimates, we can conclude that the Smoot-Hawley tariff led to about a 15 percent reduction in dutiable imports—somewhere around 13–17 percent—enough to reduce total imports by 5 percent. There is no doubt that imports were highly sensitive to changes in import duties.

Although Smoot-Hawley did cause imports to fall, the decline was relatively small when compared to the subsequent collapse in trade. U.S. foreign trade experienced its

[11] A regression analysis in which monthly dutiable imports is the dependent variable and monthly duty-free imports and a dummy variable for the Smoot-Hawley tariff period (from July 1930) are the independent variables, along with month dummies, indicates that the tariff reduced dutiable imports by about 16 percent. A few goods were transferred from the duty-free list to the dutiables list, but this would slightly understate the drop in imports as a result of the

worst ever peacetime collapse during the Great Depression. Between 1929 and 1932, the volume of imports fell 40 percent. The fall in imports was much greater than the 25 percent decline in real GDP over the same period. As a result, imports as a share of GDP fell from 4.2 percent in 1929 to 2.3 percent in 1932, and dutiable imports as a share of GDP fell from 1.4 percent to a pitiful 0.7 percent.

There are three principal reasons for the decline in imports during this period: the Smoot-Hawley tariff in 1930, the deflation-induced increase in tariffs from 1929 to 1933, and the decline in national income (real GDP) from 1929 to 1932. As figure 2.3 illustrates, the decline in the volume of imports closely tracked the decline in real GDP. Unless the tariff contributed to the fall in income, a point that will be considered later, the decline in America's demand for imported goods due to lower income appears to be the single most important factor behind the decline in imports. Indeed, the volume of imports had already fallen 15 percent in the year prior to the imposition of the Smoot-Hawley tariff (1929:Q2–1930:Q2), a period when real GDP declined 7 percent.

Counterfactual simulations using an import demand equation suggest that, of the 40 percent drop in import

---

higher duties. Hall's (1933) contemporary estimate of the tariff's impact on trade is similar. Hall divided imports into two categories—those subject to new duties as a result of 1930 legislation and those where the duties did not change. The reduction in imports in the latter category was taken to represent the impact of general trends, whereas any additional decline in imports in the former category was attributed to the tariff. During the year October 1930–September 1931, imports of goods for which the tariff did not change declined slightly more than 43 percent from their 1929 value, whereas imports of goods for which the tariff did change fell 60 percent from their 1929 value. He concluded that U.S. imports were about $190 million lower as a result of the higher tariff, implying that tariff-affected imports declined by about 17 percent, or that overall imports would have fallen by roughly 6 percent.

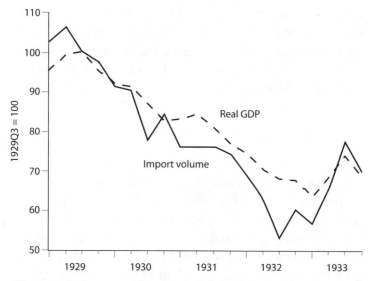

Figure 2.3. Imports volume and real GDP, quarterly, 1929–1933. Source: Real GDP, Gordon (1986); Survey of Current Business, July 1951.

volume, about 4–5 percentage points was due to the Smoot-Hawley legislation and about 8–10 percentage points due to the deflation-induced increase in the average tariff. From this we see that about 12–15 percentage points—around 30–40 percent—of the reduction in imports was due to higher tariffs and about 25–28 percentage points—about 60–70 percent—of the reduction in imports was due to lower income.[12] Thus, Smoot-Hawley by itself accounts for 10–13 percent of the decline in

[12] This is a revision of the estimate in Irwin (1998b). Over this entire period, from the second half of 1930 to the second half of 1932, the average tariff rose about 54 percent, resulting in a 15 percent increase in the relative price of imports. Roughly a third of this increase was due to the Smoot-Hawley legislation, the remaining two-thirds due to the deflation-induced increase in the burden of specific duties. The combined impact translates into a 12 percent reduction in the volume of imports.

imports during this period. Although this is a significant portion of the decline, it does not explain the entire collapse of imports. Most of the decline in imports—about two-thirds—was the result of a decline in demand resulting from falling income.

SMOOT-HAWLEY AND THE GREAT DEPRESSION

The Great Depression of the 1930s was the most severe economic downturn in U.S. history. Real GDP fell 25 percent between the business cycle peak in mid-1929 and its trough in early 1933. The civilian unemployment rate rose from 4 percent in 1929 to 23 percent in 1933. Industrial production declined 55 percent between August 1929 and March 1933. And deflation was a persistent problem; between August 1929 and March 1933, the wholesale price index slid 37 percent and farm prices plunged 64 percent. Even after the economy turned the corner in 1933, the recovery was incomplete. Another severe recession hit in 1937–38, and as late as 1939, the unemployment rate was still more than 17 percent, or 12 percent if one includes workers employed by temporary work relief programs set up by the government.[13]

Although some have supposed that the Smoot-Hawley tariff was a response to the Great Depression, this is not the case. As we have seen, preparation for a tariff revision began in late 1928 as a reaction to the economic problems farmers faced in the 1920s. This was well before the stock

---

[13] These data are from the Carter and Sutch (2006), series Ca9 and Ba475 and *Statistical Abstract of the United States* (1934, 283, 703). For a concise overview of the U.S. economy in the depression, see Romer (1993).

On the Right Door-step
—Edwards in the Akron "Times-Press."

Source: *Akron Times Press*

market crash, the slide in industrial production, and the increase in unemployment. The onset of the recession in August 1929 might have made the Senate more favorably inclined toward the legislation in early 1930, but at this point the recession was still relatively mild. As figure 2.3 shows, the economy never experienced a sudden collapse in output. Instead, output just dropped relentlessly as it was hit by a series of increasingly severe shocks: a banking panic in late 1930, more severe banking and financial problems in the fall of 1931, and finally, a continued economic slide through most of 1932 that culminated in a devastating banking crisis in early 1933.

If the Smoot-Hawley tariff was not a response to the Great Depression, was it in any way responsible for it? Did the tariff alter the declining path of real GDP? Did the Smoot-Hawley tariff intensify, ameliorate, or have no effect on the Great Depression?

The impact of the Smoot-Hawley tariff on the Great Depression is a controversial question, but there is in fact a consensus among professional economists about the answer. Most economists, both liberal and conservative, doubt that Smoot-Hawley played much of a role in the subsequent contraction. In 2006, when asked if the Smoot-Hawley tariff caused the Great Depression, the University of Chicago economist (and Nobel laureate) Milton Friedman replied:

> No. I think the Smoot-Hawley tariff was a bad law. I think it did harm. But the Smoot-Hawley tariff by itself would not have made one quarter of the labor force unemployed.[14]

Other leading economists would agree with this assessment. "The idea that the Smoot-Hawley tariff was a major cause of the Depression is an enduring conviction," Peter Temin (1989, 46) writes. "Despite its popularity, however, the argument fails on both theoretical and historical

[14] http://www.hillsdale.edu/hctools/ImprimisTool/archives/2006_07_Imprimis .pdf. Accessed June 16, 2010.

grounds." Gregory Mankiw (2009) says that the Smoot-Hawley tariff "did not cause the Great Depression, but it contributed to a plunge in world trade and undoubtedly was a step in the wrong direction." Paul Krugman (1990, 103) is unequivocal: "The claim that protectionism caused the Depression is nonsense." Robert Lucas (1994, 13) reckons that the impact of the Smoot-Hawley–sized tariff in a real business cycle model would be "trivial."

Why are most economists skeptical that the Smoot-Hawley tariff contributed very much to the Great Depression? To start, there is no reason why a tariff should necessarily trigger a depression of the magnitude seen during 1929–33. Imposing a higher tariff raises the domestic price of imported goods and changes the composition of domestic economic activity by increasing output and employment in import-competing industries and decreasing output and employment in export-oriented industries. There is no reason to think that the net effect on domestic output is wholly negative: although domestic production of goods for export will fall, domestic production of goods that substitute for imports will rise. In addition, the magnitude of the tariff shock in the Smoot-Hawley legislation, which increased the domestic price of imports by 5 percent at a time when dutiable imports were just 1.4 percent of GDP, was simply not large enough to trigger the kind of economic contraction experienced after 1930.

Historical experience bears this out. Over the course of U.S. history, import duties have changed many times without resulting in economic collapse or an economic boom. For example, the much larger Fordney-McCumber tariff increase in 1922 was actually followed by a strong economic growth. (Of course, this does not mean that the growth was due to the tariff.) Throughout history, the business cycle has had a greater impact on tariff policy than tariffs have had on the business cycle. When the economy goes into a recession, politicians often respond by raising tariffs.[15] But given that tariff changes typically have small impact on the overall U.S. economy (because they are usually modest changes in duties on imports that are a small percent of GDP), they are almost never the driving force behind the business cycle.

If the tariff was not the primary cause of the Depression, then what was? The consensus among economic historians is that monetary and financial factors were the dominant factors behind the Great Depression in the United States. Milton Friedman and Anna J. Schwartz's *A Monetary History of the United States, 1867–1960*, published in 1963, is often taken as a starting point. Friedman and Schwartz argued that the Federal Reserve, the nation's central bank, allowed the money supply to fall by about one-third from 1929 to 1933. This led to severe deflation: between December 1929 and June 1933, for example, consumer prices fell 25 percent. Deflation, in turn, meant that real interest rates were incredibly high, killing off business investment, as Romer (1992) shows. Deflation also increased the real cost of servicing debt that remained fixed in nominal terms: the ratio of debt service to national income rose from 9 percent in 1929 to nearly 20 percent in 1932–33, according to evidence cited by Bernanke (1983). This led to fi-

[15] This makes the relationship between the two easy to misinterpret. Because of the political time lag involved, the tariffs tend to get imposed near the trough of the business cycle. When the economic recovery begins, people observe the correlation of higher tariffs and economic growth and sometimes mistake it for a causal relationship. This is what happened in 1922.

nancial distress among those who had borrowed money, and the increase in non-performing loans put banks under financial pressure. The inevitable result was bank failures. This not only disrupted credit markets, but it led to large withdrawals of deposits, there being no deposit insurance, leading to further deflation. Throughout the financial turmoil of the period, the Federal Reserve did nothing to ease the situation.[16]

In particular, the decision by the Federal Reserve to raise interest rates sharply in October 1931, at a time when the economy was already perilously weak, was an enormous blow. The reason for this action can only be understood by recalling that the United States, like other major countries, was on the gold standard. The gold standard meant that the world's economies were tightly linked to each other through a regime of fixed exchange rates, which transmitted monetary and financial disturbances from one country to another. When Britain abandoned the gold standard in September 1931, the United States began to lose massive amounts of its gold reserves. The Federal Reserve responded by raising interest rates to stop the drain and keep the dollar pegged to the value of gold. In doing so, the Federal Reserve chose to maintain the exchange rate peg rather than to help the domestic economy. This led to more deflation and additional bank failures, which only intensified the depression.

Most economists believe that if the Federal Reserve had taken more aggressive action to stop the bank failures and

[16] On Federal Reserve policy, see Friedman and Schwartz (1963) and Meltzer (2003). Federal Reserve policy makers had an erroneous view of the economy (the real bills doctrine) in which they interpreted low nominal interest rates as indicating that monetary policy was easy.

counteract the decline in the money supply, the Great Depression could have been avoided.[17] But the fact that the United States was on a gold standard constrained what it could do, or what it thought it could do.[18] In fact, the U.S. economy did not begin to recover and the deflation did not end until President Franklin Roosevelt took the country off the gold standard in April 1933 (Temin and Wigmore 1990; Eggertsson 2008). More than any other factor, an expansionary monetary policy was the key to the economic recovery after 1933, and getting off the gold standard was a critical part of this policy shift (Romer 1992).

In sum, there are no strong theoretical or empirical grounds for believing that higher average tariffs are the principal cause of business cycle downturns or expansions. In addition, monetary and financial factors were of overwhelming importance in generating the Great Depression.[19]

But even if it did not cause the Great Depression, could the Smoot-Hawley tariff have affected the course of the

[17] For example, the economy began to stabilize in mid-1932 as the Federal Reserve began to ease monetary policy, but it quickly reversed course for fear of sparking inflation and the economy started deteriorating once again. Richardson and Troost (2009) show that the Federal Reserve could have done something to prevent banking panics.

[18] There is a debate among economic historians about the extent to which Federal Reserve policy actions were actually constrained by the gold standard. Temin (1989) and Eichengreen (1992) emphasize the gold standard constraint on monetary policy and argue that the gold standard played a large role in making the Great Depression an international phenomenon. Bordo, Choudhri, and Schwartz (2002) and Hsieh and Romer (2006) argue that the Federal Reserve had enough gold reserves so that it could have pursued a more expansionary monetary policy if it had chosen to.

[19] Friedman and Schwartz (1963) scarcely mention the Smoot-Hawley tariff in their seminal chapter on the monetary factors behind the Depression. Schwartz (1981, 22) later argued that "the decline in U.S. lending abroad and the protectionist Smoot-Hawley Tariff Act were clearly U.S. actions that destabilized the world financial system," but provided no elaboration.

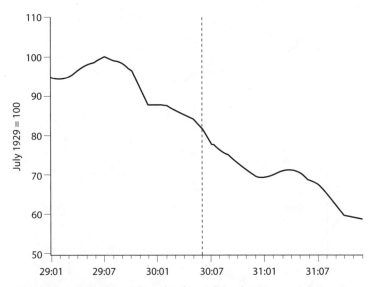

Figure 2.4. Monthly index of industrial production, 1929–1931 (seasonally adjusted). Source: http://www.federalreserve.gov/Releases/g17/iphist/iphist_sa.txt.

Depression? One check on whether Smoot-Hawley had any discernable impact on the Depression is simply to look at various economic indicators, such as industrial production and farm prices, before and after the tariff was imposed. Figure 2.4 depicts the Federal Reserve's monthly index of industrial production. The slide in industrial output was well under way when the tariff was enacted in late June 1930, and there is no noticeable change after the tariff was imposed. The tariff did not arrest the decline, but neither did it accelerate the decline. (This is not unexpected, given that the scope for increasing domestic output by decreasing imports was slight.)

Figure 2.5 shows a monthly index of farm prices. There was a sharp drop in farm prices in July 1930, the month

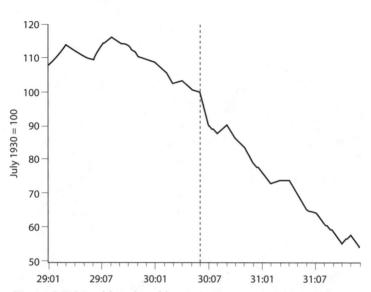

Figure 2.5. Monthly index of farm prices, 1929–1931. Source: *Statistical Abstract of the United States* 1933, 279.

after the Smoot-Hawley tariff took effect. Whether this can be attributed to the tariff or other factors is not clear. One financial publication at the time reported: "There were no special developments to account for the renewed break in the market value of wheat and the further depreciation appeared to result entirely from the fact that the large wheat holdings of the Federal Farm Board and its subsidiaries were hanging over the market and that the new winter wheat crop in this country was about to come to market in considerable quantity" (*The Annalist*, July 1930, 6). But the tariff does not appear to have affected the overall trend of declining farm prices.

Of course, with so many different shocks hitting the economy, it is difficult to isolate the contribution of the Smoot-Hawley tariff. It is commonly thought to have exacerbated the slump by destroying trade. Yet some economists have suggested that the tariff might have ameliorated the Depression by providing a short-run stimulus to the economy. Rudiger Dornbusch and Stanley Fischer (1986, 468–69) argue that a tariff might have helped the economy because "from either a Keynesian or a monetarist perspective, the tariff by itself would have been an expansionary impulse in the absence of retaliation. In the Keynesian view, the reduction in imports diverts demand to domestic goods; in the monetarist view the gold inflow increases the domestic money stock if not sterilized." Because the United States had a fixed exchange rate, both of these channels were potentially operative.

To explore this possibility, we will consider three frameworks—Keynesian, monetarist, and real business cycle—as well as several other potential channels for understanding the possible macroeconomic effects of the tariff.

THE KEYNESIAN APPROACH

In the Keynesian view, an increase in tariffs will shift domestic expenditures from foreign goods to domestic goods, thereby increasing domestic output at the expense of foreign output. This is known as expenditure switching. The Keynesian approach is sometimes explained with reference to the national income accounting identity:

$$Y = C + I + G + (X - M) \qquad (2.1)$$

where Y is national income (GDP), C is consumption expenditures, I is investment expenditures, G is government expenditures, and $X - M$ is net exports (exports minus imports).[20] In this setup, anything that diminishes imports—reducing M—will raise income, all other things being equal. If the tariff reduces spending on imports without adversely affecting exports, an important qualification, then net exports increase and contribute to a more-than-proportionate increase in aggregate demand for domestic goods due to the multiplier effect. However, if exports fall as much as imports, then net exports do not change and there is no stimulative effect on aggregate demand.[21]

Yet the scope for expenditure switching through a higher tariff was extremely limited. The Smoot-Hawley tariff reduced imports by about 0.2 percent of GDP. The elasticity of substitution between imported and domestic goods was probably very low; because of the existing high tariff, only specialty products that were not good substitutes for U.S. products were imported. Both of these factors—the small amount of spending on imports as a percent of GDP and the low elasticity of substitution between domestic and foreign goods—imply that the kick to domestic output from reducing imports would have been very limited.

[20] Exports are foreign demand for domestic goods and services, while imports are deducted because some of the other components of domestic spending, such as consumption, include imported goods.

[21] While this identity is useful for thinking about some issues, it can be quite misleading in understanding the benefits of trade. For example, if a reduction in trade costs or in trade barriers allows trade to expand, both exports and imports might rise by the same amount, leading to no change in income in the context of this identity. Yet there could be significant welfare benefits to this trade that are not captured in this accounting framework. To take an extreme example, if international trade were eliminated entirely, putting both exports and imports to zero, measured national income would supposedly remain unchanged, assuming no changes to C or I or G. But those components would surely be affected by the loss of trade, perhaps with devastating economic consequences. We will return to this issue later in the chapter.

In one simulation, Eichengreen (1989) uses a Keynesian-type model to suggest that the expenditure-switching effect of the Smoot-Hawley tariff could have increased domestic output by 5 percent, in the absence of foreign retaliation. Even with a large multiplier effect, this seems an implausibly large effect given that dutiable imports were 1.4 percent of GDP in 1929. After incorporating limited foreign retaliation into the model, Eichengreen finds a smaller but still positive net expansionary effect from Smoot-Hawley—about 2 percent of GDP. Eichengreen (1989, 36) concludes that, "whether or not one agrees with the particulars of this analysis, it is hard to dispute that the direct macroeconomic effects of the Smoot-Hawley tariff, operating primarily through the volume of trade, were small relative to the Great Depression."

These simulation results notwithstanding, there is no direct empirical evidence that the Smoot-Hawley tariff produced any stimulus via expenditure switching. If that was the case, imports should have declined more than exports and real net exports would have contributed (in an accounting sense) to growth. Figure 2.6 shows that the opposite was the case: exports fell even more than imports. While the volume of imports fell 12 percent between 1930 and 1931, the volume of exports fell 19 percent. While the volume of imports fell 40 percent between 1929 and 1932, the volume of exports fell 49 percent. As a result, with the exception of one year, real net exports were a drag on the economy from 1930 through 1936, providing no boost to aggregate demand (table 2.2). The implication is that trends in exports and imports worsened the Depression, but only by a small amount.

What accounts for the enormous drop in U.S. exports? The declining demand for U.S. exports could have been

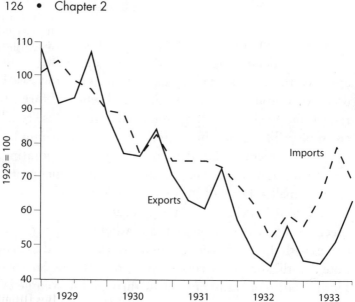

Figure 2.6. Volume of exports and imports, by quarter, 1929–1933.
Source: *Survey of Current Business*, July 1951, 27.

caused by several factors. These include: (1) the greater
obstacles faced by foreign countries seeking to earn dollars from their exports to the United States; (2) declining
foreign incomes due to the Great Depression abroad; (3)
higher foreign tariffs and other trade restrictions aimed
directly or indirectly at the United States; (4) the real appreciation of the dollar as other countries (notably Britain) left the gold standard and allowed their currencies to
depreciate against the dollar.

All of these factors are likely to have played a role. The
claim that Smoot-Hawley exacerbated world trade tensions and led directly to these higher foreign trade barriers will be examined in more detail in chapter 3, but
Dornbusch and Fischer (1986, 469) note that in 1929, exports were 5 percent of GDP, whereas by 1931, they had

TABLE 2.2.
Percentage Contribution to Change in Real GNP, 1930–1939

	Real GNP	Consumption	Investment	Inventories	Government	Exports	Imports	Net exports
1930	9.9	4.4	6.3	-2.0	1.1	-0.7	0.6	0.0
1931	7.7	2.4	5.8	-1.0	0.6	-0.8	0.6	0.2
1932	14.8	6.8	7.2	-2.3	0.7	-1.1	0.8	0.3
1933	-1.9	-1.4	0.4	1.4	-0.7	0.0	-0.4	-0.4
1934	9.0	3.9	3.0	1.2	2.4	0.1	0.0	0.1
1935	9.9	4.9	5.7	3.4	0.3	0.3	-1.1	-0.8
1936	13.9	7.5	3.5	0.4	2.8	0.3	-0.3	-0.1
1937	5.3	2.4	3.0	1.2	-0.5	0.8	-0.6	0.2
1938	-5.1	-1.4	-6.2	-3.8	1.5	0.0	1.2	1.2
1939	8.6	4.2	3.4	1.9	0.7	0.1	-0.4	-0.3

Source: U.S. Department of Commerce (1976), series F 47–70.
Note: Components may not sum to real GNP due to rounding and statistical discrepancy.

fallen to 1.5 percent of GDP. Attributing the entire fall to foreign retaliation and assuming a multiplier effect of two, they suggest that the decline in real net exports would have reduced real GDP by 3 percent. Even if we accept this overestimate, it is still a small part of the 15 percent decline in real GDP between 1929 and 1931. Thus, the deteriorating world trade environment, to some extent the result of Smoot-Hawley, could have played a role in exacerbating the Great Depression. Still, to explain the situation fully, we need to look elsewhere.

Table 2.3 provides a summary of changes in domestic demand and real net exports over three key periods. The fall in real net exports between 1930 and 1933 exacerbated the Great Depression to a slight degree. The fall in real net exports is surprising because the Great Depression was much more severe in the United States than in other countries; usually a country that suffers a more serious downturn than its trading partners will see its exports hold up while its imports fall off. The fall in real net exports between 1933 and 1936 is also surprising. Even though the dollar depreciated against other major currencies after the United States left the gold standard in April 1933, real net exports continued to be a drag on GDP growth.[22]

To conclude, whatever plausible, positive Keynesian-type effects might have arisen by reducing imports via the tariff were more than offset by declining exports. As a result, developments in U.S. foreign trade exacerbated the Depression slightly and hindered the recovery slightly. As chapter 3 will discuss, there is evidence that trade policy

[22] Bernanke (1995) finds that the exports of countries going off the gold standard grew more rapidly than the exports of countries remaining on the gold standard.

TABLE 2.3.
Percentage Contribution to Change in Real GNP,
Selected Periods

Period	Real GNP	Domestic demand	Net exports
1930–1933	−25.0	−24.3	−0.8
1933–1936	+43.1	+43.9	−0.8
1936–1939	+6.7	+5.5	+1.2

Source: U.S. Department of Commerce (1976), series F 47-70.

measures in other countries aimed at the United States
as a result of the Smoot-Hawley tariff contributed to this
outcome.

The Monetarist Approach

According to the monetarist view, an increase in the tariff
leads to a decrease in imports with no immediate change
in exports. This trade surplus generates an inflow of gold
and an expansion of the money supply that gives the
economy a short-run stimulus. Eventually, however, the
monetary expansion leads to higher domestic prices. This
will reduce exports, increase imports, and restore the bal-
ance of trade to its original position, other things being
equal.

We can assess the monetary impact of the Smoot-Hawley tariff by looking at whether gold imports increased in
the months after its imposition. The data in figure 2.7 do
not show any large increase in U.S. gold imports after
the tariff was implemented. In July and August 1930, immediately after the tariff took effect, the United States

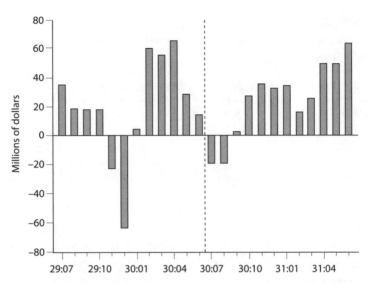

Figure 2.7. Monthly net gold imports, July 1929–June 1931. Source: Monthly Summary of the Foreign Commerce of the United States, July 1931.

actually exported large amounts of gold (about $40 million), mainly to France and Canada. The United States was a net importer of gold for the rest of the year, but not outside the usual range. If the Smoot-Hawley tariff did encourage the importation of gold, it is not immediately evident in the data.[23]

---

[23] Friedman and Schwartz (1963, 342) report that stock of high-powered money rose by $340 million between October 1930 and January 1931. They attribute this rise to an increase of $117 million in outstanding Federal Reserve credit and an inflow of $84 million in gold, which they assign partly to the Smoot-Hawley tariff, a reduction in U.S. lending abroad, and other factors. Yet the stock of money declined by more than 3 percent over this period due to the onset of the first banking crisis, which sharply reduced the ratio of deposits to currency. Thus, even if the Smoot-Hawley tariff contributed in some degree to the gold inflows in the months after it was imposed, it was completely swamped by other factors.

Significant gold inflows would have helped stimulate the economy, unless the central bank sterilized the inflow by taking offsetting policy actions to leave monetary conditions unchanged. In fact, that was precisely the Federal Reserve's policy at the time. As Friedman and Schwartz (1963, 282) note, "From 1923 on, gold movements were largely offset by movements in Federal Reserve credit so that there was essentially no relation between the movements of gold and in the total of high powered money; the fairly irregular dips and rises in the gold stock were transformed into a horizontal movement in total high powered money." For example, in July and August 1930, the Federal Reserve sterilized the gold outflow. As it explained: "The loss of gold was without effect on money market conditions in the United States, either in July or in August, as it was offset in July by the inflow of currency from circulation and in August by open-market operations of the Federal reserve banks" (*Federal Reserve Bulletin*, September 1930, 534–35). Hence, even if the tariff had led to substantial gold inflows, the Federal Reserve's policy of sterilizing changes in gold reserves would have prevented the inflows from affecting monetary conditions.

If the tariff had led to an inflow of gold from the rest of the world and the Federal Reserve had neutralized its domestic expansionary impact, other countries would have lost gold reserves to the United States. This would have forced them to pursue more deflationary policies, without receiving any compensatory increase in exports from a more expansionary U.S. monetary policy. For this reason, Alan Meltzer (1976, 469–70) believes the Smoot-Hawley tariff played a significant role in the onset of the Depression. He contends that it "worked to convert a sizeable recession into a severe depression" since it "increased the deflationary impulse" around the world by increasing the stock of monetary gold in the United States, thus leading to tighter monetary policies abroad without producing a monetary expansion at home.[24]

As already pointed out, one problem with this argument is that there was no apparent increase in U.S. gold inflows after the tariff was imposed. Furthermore, the argument that the United States transmitted the Depression to the rest of the world by hoarding gold reserves is suspect because gold reserves in the rest of the world did not decline for most of the depression period (Fremling 1985). This is also true around the time that the Smoot-Hawley tariff was imposed. Although U.S. gold reserves were 1.1 percent higher in December 1930 than they had been in June of that year (the month the Smoot-Hawley tariff was imposed), the gold reserves of foreign central banks increased 2.9 percent (*Federal Reserve Bulletin*, June 1933, 368). This is inconsistent with the United States drawing gold to itself at the expense of the rest of the world immediately following Smoot-Hawley.

More plausibly, Meltzer suggests that the Smoot-Hawley tariff and foreign retaliation harmed U.S. agricultural exports, thereby reducing farm prices and leading to mortgage defaults and bank failures in farm states

[24]Meltzer (1976, 460) explains his argument this way: "The tariffs restricted the operation of the price-specie flow mechanism and the adjustment of the U.S. and the world economy. In the absence of the tariff, prices in the U.S. would have fallen relative to prices abroad, and the change in relative prices would have increased foreign demand and net exports. With the tariff in effect during 1930 . . . monetary gold stock increased, and prices in the U.S. fell by less than prices in other industrial countries. . . . This argument assigns a large role to the Hawley-Smoot tariff and subsequent tariff retaliation in explaining why the 1929 recession did not follow the path of previous monetary contractions but became the Great Depression."

in 1930 and 1931. As Meltzer (1976, 461) states: "given the size of the decline in food exports and in agricultural prices, it is not surprising that many of the U.S. banks that failed in 1930 and in 1931 were in agricultural regions."[25] Thus, the agricultural regions harmed by restrictive trade measures abroad were the initial source of the banking problems that then spread to other parts of the country.[26]

There is no doubt that falling agricultural prices led to tremendous farm distress and contributed to the financial weakness of rural banks. It is also true that, in November and December 1930 and January 1931, just months after the passage of the Smoot-Hawley tariff, there was a sharp rise in bank failures. But can these events be attributed to the Smoot-Hawley tariff? It turns out that there was another factor at work—a severe drought in the late summer of 1930. This drought aggravated the desperate agricultural situation in the south-central United States. "The disastrous effects of the low yields and low prices help explain why the drought and cotton states and not the western grain states had the most bank failures in 1930," Hamilton (1985, 604) notes. "Of the nine states that had large increases in failures, five—Arkansas, Mississippi, Alabama, North Carolina, and Tennessee—were heavily dependent on cotton income, and at least seven—Arkansas, Mississippi, Kentucky, Missouri, Tennessee, Illinois,

[25] Meltzer (2003, 564) later noted that "Most research suggesting a small effect [from the Smoot-Hawley tariff] ignores the pronounced effect on farm exports, distress, bankruptcies, and bank failures in farm states."

[26] In discussing the banking crisis of late 1930, Friedman and Schwartz (1963, 308) write: "A crop of bank failures, particularly in Missouri, Indiana, Illinois, Iowa, Arkansas, and North Carolina, led to widespread attempts to convert demand and time deposits into currency . . . A contagion of fear spread among depositors, starting from the agricultural areas, which had experienced the heaviest impact of bank failures in the 1920s."

and Indiana—suffered extensive drought damage."[27] Since rural banks depended on high land values and commodity prices to maintain the value of their loan portfolio, the combination of low yields and world prices led to a sudden loss of deposits and a rise in non-performing loans, putting banks under great financial pressure.

If declining foreign demand was responsible for the problems agricultural producers faced, and hence the banking problems in late 1930, we would expect to see declining domestic production, increasing domestic consumption, and decreasing exports. Yet data on U.S. agricultural production and trade do not support this story. As table 2.4 shows, the drought and declining domestic demand seems to explain what happened to cotton in 1930. Cotton production fell 6 percent in 1930, presumably because of the drought. But domestic demand from America's textile mills fell even more, by nearly 16 percent, because of the recession. As a result, cotton exports and the share of cotton exported actually increased in 1930.

In the case of wheat and tobacco, exports did fall in 1930, but that appears to be due to domestic demand growing more rapidly than domestic production grew. In the case of corn, the drought slashed domestic production and consumption and the role of trade was negligible.

There are other reasons for being skeptical of the argument that the Smoot-Hawley tariff was responsible for a decline in agricultural exports and prices that in turn led to farm bankruptcies, and hence to rural bank

[27] In his study of banking crises during the Great Depression, Wicker (1996, 51) notes that "the devastating agricultural drought in the South during the summer of 1930 played an important ancillary role in accounting for the high incidence of bank suspensions in primarily agricultural regions."

TABLE 2.4.
Agricultural Production and Exports

	Production	Exports	Imports	Consumption	Exports/Production (percent)
Cotton (thousands of bales)					
1929	14,828	7,035	395	8,188	47.4
1930	13,932	7,133	112	6,911	51.2
Percentage change	−6.0	+1.3	−71.6	−15.6	—
Wheat (thousands of bushels)					
1929	812,573	153,245	12,956	672,284	18.9
1930	857,427	131,475	19,059	745,011	15.3
Percentage change	+5.5	−14.2	+47.1	+10.8	
Tobacco (thousands of pounds)					
1929	1,537,313	600,181	63,181	1,000,313	39.0
1930	1,647,377	591,035	75,425	1,121,767	35.9
Percentage change	+7.2	−1.5	+19.4	+13.1	
Corn (thousands of bushels)					
1929	2,535,386	10,281	497	2,525,602	0.4
1930	2,059,641	3,317	1,747	2,058,071	0.2
Percentage change	−18.8	−67.7	+151.1	−18.5	

Source: U.S. Department of Agriculture, *Yearbook of Agriculture 1933.*
Note: Exports and imports for year beginning in July (August in the case of cotton).

failures. In terms of the banking crisis of 1930, the major bank failure had little to do with declining exports and a lot to do with bad management practices. The failure of Caldwell & Co. in Nashville, Tennessee, a major bank in the southeast, was not due to agriculture's problems. Instead, Hamilton (1985, 591) finds that "reckless expansion, careless management, and unethical practices on the part of the firm's officers were almost entirely responsible for its demise." Furthermore, although the banking panics were concentrated in agricultural regions, there is little evidence that they had contagion effects leading to similar banking problems in the East. White (1984, 120) notes that the banking crisis of late 1930 "did not mark the change from a recession to a depression" and "was primarily regional in nature and had little impact on the national economy." Instead, it "appears to be a part of the economic downturn rather than a major turning point in the depression."

There are other problems with the idea that Smoot-Hawley led to a cascade of effects that contributed to the nation's financial woes. The rate of farm foreclosure was no higher in 1930 or 1931 than it had been in the late 1920s; only as the severity of the depression intensified in 1932 and 1933 did foreclosures reach the incredible rates of 28 percent and 39 percent, respectively (Alston 1983). And while farm exports did suffer enormously in 1931 and thereafter, by this time many other events had taken place, especially the Federal Reserve's tightening of credit in the fall of 1931 when Britain left the gold standard. Finally, as chapter 3 will discuss, when foreign countries retaliated against the United States for imposing the Smoot-Hawley tariff, they usually struck back against American exports of manufactured goods, such as automobiles, rather than its exports of agricultural goods.

In sum, the Smoot-Hawley tariff did not lead to any pronounced increase in gold inflows. Even if it had, the Federal Reserve's policy of sterilizing gold flows meant that it would not have had any stimulative effect on the economy. And given the modest effects of the Smoot-Hawley tariff on imports and prices, it is unlikely that it was a powerful enough force to have triggered a widespread agricultural collapse and the associated banking problems.[28]

The Real Business Cycle Approach

Economists have recently developed calibrated neoclassical equilibrium growth models to assess the impact of various shocks—monetary, productivity, tax, and so forth—on output and employment over time. These models are sometimes called "real business cycle" models because they tend to emphasize the impact of productivity shocks on output. They focus on how deviations from equilibrium conditions among producers and consumers, and the allocation of output between consumption and investment, can affect economic fluctuations.[29] In the

---

[28] The role of agriculture in the Great Depression is still debated. Madsen (2001a) finds that agricultural prices were a mechanism for transmitting the Depression around the world, while Federico (2005) argues that agriculture was more harmed by the Depression than an independent cause of it.

[29] In these models, producers must choose the optimal amounts of capital and labor to use in production, as well as the aggregate production technology. Consumers must make a choice about time allocation and labor supply between market production and leisure.

context of these models, University of Chicago economist Robert Lucas (1994, 13) has contended:

> It would be a term-paper-size exercise, for example, to work out the possible effects of the 1930 Smoot-Hawley Tariff in a suitably adapted real business cycle model. By now, we have accumulated enough quantitative experience with such models to be sure that the aggregate effects of such a policy (in an economy with a 5% foreign trade sector before the Act and perhaps a percentage point less after) would be trivial.

Cole and Ohanian (1999, 2007) have applied such models to the Great Depression in the United States and conclude that, just as Lucas suspected, "tariffs were not an important factor for either the decline phase or the weak recovery" of the 1930s.

Yet Crucini and Kahn (1996, 2007) argue that, even though the effect of tariffs may be small in the context of the Great Depression, it can still generate a recession-size effect. They develop a model in which imports are treated as intermediate goods and therefore tariffs on those imports create a production distortion that reduces the marginal product of labor. By reducing the capital stock, this inefficiency has a persistent, negative effect on the economy. Crucini and Kahn (2007) report that higher tariffs could have reduced output between 2 percent and 5 percent, far from the 25 percent decline in output observed during the Great Depression but still fairly substantial. Hence, the authors conclude that trade policy can have significant macroeconomic effects if we consider trade in intermediate goods (those used in production) and the dynamics of capital accumulation and labor supply that result from a permanent change in the tariff, as well as foreign retaliation.

However, the dynamic response of the capital stock accounts for most of the simulation's finding. If the capital stock is assumed to be fixed, the impact of higher tariffs is much smaller, ranging from 0.8 percent loss of output to a 1.9 percent gain to output. Furthermore, Cole and Ohanian note that these results arise from some special assumptions in the model, particularly the treatment of all imports as intermediate rather than final goods and the assumption of a low elasticity of substitution between imported and domestic intermediate goods, which magnifies the impact of disrupting imports. In fact, about 55 percent of U.S. imports in 1929 were intermediate goods for industry, 23 percent were finished manufactured goods, and 22 percent were foodstuffs. Of the intermediate goods, about 80 percent were duty-free and were unaffected by the Smoot-Hawley tariff increase.[30] Because most of the Smoot-Hawley increases were on final goods, and most of the imported intermediates remained duty-free, it is unlikely that the channels identified in the real business cycle model were an important source of the decline in output.

ALTERNATIVE CHANNELS

Finally, there are a few other mechanisms by which the Smoot-Hawley tariff might have affected the course of the Great Depression. One is simply that increased trade

[30] The intermediate goods are classified as crude materials and semi-manufactures. *Statistical Abstract of the United States* 1931, 495–97.

tends to increase national income, whereas higher tariffs destroy trade and can reduce income. If that is the case, how much did the destruction of trade feed back and reduce income?[31]

To determine how much the elimination of trade might reduce income, we need an estimate of how much an exogenous change in trade changes income. Feyrer (2009) uses time-varying distances between countries as a way of identifying the impact of trade on income and finds that a 1 percent increase in trade leads to about a 0.5 percent increase in income. As noted earlier in the chapter, the Smoot-Hawley tariff reduced dutiable imports by about 16 percent. If dutiable imports fell 16 percent in 1929, it would have destroyed $233 million in trade that year. This implies that by reducing trade, the Smoot-Hawley tariff reduced America's income by $116 million annually, or 0.1 percent of 1929 GDP. Adding the deflation-induced increase in the tariff as well, higher tariffs would have eliminated $700 million in 1929 trade, reducing income by 0.3 percent of 1929 GDP. Although this is an imperfect comparison, because an increase in tariffs is not the same as an exogenous increase in trade costs, it does appear that the reduction in trade did not reduce income enough to account for much of the Depression.

Another contention is that Congress's lengthy consideration of the tariff bill contributed to business un-

[31] As noted earlier, the Keynesian model implicit in equation (2.1) is ill-equipped to deal with this issue because a complete elimination of trade would supposedly have no effect on GDP. In addition, this reduction in income is more than the simple static deadweight loss resulting from a higher tax on imports, which one would expect to be small. The static welfare losses associated with the Smoot-Hawley tariff were probably very small, certainly in comparison to the magnitude of the Depression. One estimate suggests that the deadweight welfare losses associated with the U.S. tariff structure increased by 0.1 percent of GDP between 1929 and 1933 (Irwin 2010).

certainty, which led to the postponement of investment and the slide into recession. As table 2.2 shows, declining investment was a major contributor of the economic collapse in the early 1930s, mainly because of high real interest rates. However, the resolution of this uncertainty about the tariff after June 1930 does not appear to have helped the economy very much. Archibald and Feldman (1998) investigated the relationship between an industry's international exposure and its investment spending to see if increased cash-flow uncertainty due to the tariff could have depressed investment. They found that international exposure may have played a small role in explaining investment behavior at the start of the downturn (1929) but not in later years (1930–33).

Still another argument is that, by restricting the exports of European and Latin American countries to the United States, the tariff made it more difficult for those countries to earn dollars and service their debts. This may have disrupted the international financial system and might have forced foreign countries to default on their World War I loans. Carey (1999) examined changes in prices of foreign sovereign dollar bonds over several weeks in 1930, when the Smoot-Hawley bill finally appeared to be close to passage. To determine whether the market anticipated any debt repayment problems arising from the tariffs, he compared bond price data to various indicators of a country's sensitivity to tariffs and debt service. Even though he found a significant relationship between these indicators and bond price changes in June 1930, the size of the effect was extremely small. In addition, many Latin American countries exported commodities and raw materials that came into the United States duty-free and hence were unaffected by the higher tariff.

Conclusion

The Smoot-Hawley tariff had a dramatic effect on imports of dutiable goods, reducing them by about 16 percent upon impact. Because two-thirds of imports were duty-free, total imports fell by a smaller amount—about 5 percent. The adverse effect of the tariff on trade was intensified by deflation, which significantly raises the average tariff on dutiable imports through its effect on specific duties. In all, higher tariffs account for about a third of the observed 40 percent reduction in U.S. imports during the 1929–32 period.

The more controversial question is the role of the tariff in the Great Depression. The consensus among economists is that the Smoot-Hawley tariff did not cause the Depression. The effect of the tariff was relatively minor in comparison to the powerful contractionary forces at work through the monetary and financial system. When set next to a one-third decline in the money supply, even a substantial change in tariff policy would have been unlikely to produce any major macroeconomic effects, particularly when dutiable imports were a mere 1.4 percent of GDP in 1929.

The tariff might have played a small role in either ameliorating or exacerbating the Depression. Yet neither the Keynesian nor the monetarist channels through which the tariff might have provided a short-run stimulus to the economy appears to have been at work during this period. The Keynesian channel was rendered inoperative by declining exports, while the monetarist channel was stymied by the sterilization policy of the Federal Reserve. Because exports fell more than imports, trade as a whole made the Depression worse, if only to a slight degree. The Smoot-

Hawley tariff was responsible, in some degree, for this adverse outcome. As the next chapter will show, the decline in U.S. exports was partly the result of retaliatory trade measures in other countries that were spawned by Smoot-Hawley itself.

Chapter 3
Foreign Retaliation

In the three years after the Smoot-Hawley tariff was enacted, protectionist trade measures proliferated, world trade collapsed, and the Depression intensified around the world. Smoot-Hawley's contribution to this economic disaster has been debated ever since. While the tariff was clearly a step in the direction of higher trade barriers, it was not responsible for most of the spread of protectionism around the world in the early 1930s. However, the Smoot-Hawley tariff was very damaging from the standpoint of U.S. commerce because it led other countries to pursue trade policies that explicitly discriminated against the United States. This discrimination was much more harmful to U.S. exports than simply the rise in foreign trade barriers because it diverted existing trade away from the United States and gave it to other countries. In addition, Smoot-Hawley damaged the economies of neighboring countries and this, in turn, led to political changes that were contrary to American interests, particularly the fall of pro-American governments in both Canada and Cuba.

Congress's Assessment of the Foreign Response

In enacting the Smoot-Hawley tariff, members of Congress considered only its immediate impact on their producer constituents. The well-being of the overall economy or the potential retribution by foreign countries rarely entered the discussion. While there are twenty pages of debate in the *Congressional Record* on the import duty to be imposed on tomatoes, there is very little consideration of the international reaction to the higher tariffs.

As the bill worked its way through Congress, many foreign governments and industry associations objected to the legislation. The foreign protests began arriving as early as the spring of 1929, when Congress began to consider the tariff revision. In the House Ways and Means Committee report on the bill, the Republican majority acknowledged but dismissed the concerns of foreign countries, noting: "Foreign nations and producers have shown great interest in this readjustment, but since the tariff is a domestic matter, neither foreign officials nor the nationals of foreign nations were heard [by the committee], except that representations of foreign governments were submitted through the State Department and made a part of our record. . . . We appreciate the importance of our relations to foreign countries . . . but we have believed that our first duty was to our own people and to maintenance of their prosperity" (House Report No. 7, 71st Congress, 1st Session, 6).

On the House floor, Republicans downplayed any adverse foreign reaction and said the views of foreigners should not be taken into account. Rep. Edward Browne (R-WI) argued: "the markets of the United States are for the producers of the United States . . . this is a domestic question. No matter what foreign countries think about our tariff and the tariff duties, it is a question for the people of the United States to decide" (*Congressional Record*, May 20, 1929, 1562). Democrats responded that the potential retaliation by foreign countries against U.S. exports was yet another reason to oppose the bill. As the Senate was completing its consideration of the bill, Democrats and progressive Republicans requested that the Hoover administration report all of the relevant foreign protests that had been filed with the State Department. There were enough to fill an entire book, published as volume 18 of the Senate Finance Committee hearings. The administration reported that, as of September 5, 1929, fifty-nine protests had been received from more than thirty countries. Some were officially from foreign governments, but many more were from foreign industry associations that exported to the United States. Roughly three hundred proposed tariff increases were singled out as detrimental.[1] Some even hinted that retaliatory actions might be taken against American exports. Another forty-two protests by foreign governments and businesses were received after the September date (*Congressional Record*, June 9, 1930, 10291–98).

[1] The countries were Argentina, Austria, Australia, Belgium, Bermuda, Britain, Czechoslovakia, Denmark, Dominica, the Dominican Republic, Finland, France, Germany, Greece, Guatemala, Honduras, India, Ireland, Italy, Japan, Latvia, Mexico, the Netherlands, Norway, Paraguay, Persia, Portugal, Romania, Spain, Sweden, Switzerland, Turkey, and Uruguay.

Democrats pointed to the collection as an ominous sign. As Sen. Pat Harrison (D-MS) stated:

> I hold in my hand—and I want to call it to the attention of the chairman of the Finance Committee—a book of 255 pages of small type that contains the protests of practically every government in the world against some provision of this tariff bill. Retaliations are threatened. . . . Such proposals as this tariff do not bring people closer to us nor make them more friendly with us. (*Congressional Record*, September 13, 1929, 3592–93)

Sen. Furnifold Simmons (D-NC) added:

> This bill invites not only protests—many have already come from some of our best customers among the nations, couched in diplomatic terms, of course, but nevertheless of menacing import—but it would tend to provoke retaliations and create a psychology among our foreign purchasers which would be inimical if not destructive to our commercial relations with them. Manifestly, we cannot reduce to a minimum our imports from foreign countries without eventually reducing relatively our exports to such countries. (*Congressional Record*, September 12, 1929, 3543)

As chapter 1 recounted, Old Guard Republicans opposed an export debenture for agricultural goods on the

MORE THAN HE EXPECTED

A bombardment of abuse is the heritage of Uncle Sam, who seems
sadly annoyed by the volley of bricks. An Irish cartoon attack
upon America is unusual, for the Free State and its inhabitants are
grateful for past favors.

From the *Independent* (Dublin, Irish Free State)

Source: *The Independent* (Ireland). Reprinted with permission of Independent Newspapers (Ireland).

grounds that foreign countries would simply negate it with countervailing duties. But they seemed unconcerned about the possibility that foreign countries would retaliate against the higher tariffs by raising their duties on U.S. exports. Republicans continued to insist that the tariff was a domestic measure and dismissed the possibility of an adverse foreign response as hypothetical. They maintained that the tariff legislation was purely a domestic policy measure and condemned foreign comments as an intrusion on U.S. sovereignty. "The tariff is a domestic matter, and an American tariff must be framed and put into force by the American Congress and administration," Smoot argued. "No foreign country has a right to interfere" (*Congressional Record*, September 12, 1929, 3548).

As the legislation approached completion, American exporters began to worry publicly that they would be singled out for retribution if the tariff bill became law. The automobile industry was the most concerned about being targeted by foreign countries. Both Henry Ford (of Ford Motor Co.) and Alfred Sloan (of General Motors) warned that auto exports would be hit with higher foreign duties, which would lead to adverse consequences for domestic output and employment.

In the final debate over passage, Republicans and Democrats traded charges about the international repercussions of Smoot-Hawley. Rep. Frank Crowther (R-NY) argued that only domestic considerations were at stake:

> These rates were made for the benefit of the farmers of the United States. We are not writing a tariff bill for Canada, we are writing it for the United States of America. We do not interfere with other nations when they amend their tariff act. (*Congressional Record*, June 14, 1930, 10788)

Sen. Elmer Thomas (D-OK) painted a bleak picture of the consequences:

It is stated in many places that if the pending tariff bill shall become a law it will be a declaration of economic warfare against the other nations of the world. It remains to be seen whether or not the challenge will be accepted. If this bill shall be enacted, it will further embitter our international trade relations; if this bill shall pass it will bring about additional reprisals. (*Congressional Record*, June 9, 1930, 10299)

"We have every reason to expect retaliation from other nations that may be so affected by our tariff policies," added Sen. William Brock (D-TN). "While I believe in reasonable and just protection, I am not in favor of a protective tariff which would be equivalent to an embargo and justification for retaliation by other countries" (*Congressional Record*, June 9, 1930, 10300).

THE FOREIGN REACTION TO SMOOT-HAWLEY

Although America's trading partners had been dismayed whenever the United States increased its import tariffs in the past, retaliatory responses were rare. But after World War I, the United States became the world's economic and financial leader. It represented a larger part of the world economy, and its policy actions had greater repercussions around the world. Still, when the United States imposed the Fordney-McCumber tariff in 1922, the foreign reaction was relatively muted. This is because, by the time the new American tariff was implemented, the United States had rebounded from a sharp recession and the economy was growing rapidly. Because of the strong recovery, European exports were growing at a steady pace, which masked any disruption that the tariffs caused. In addition, because the United States was lending large amounts of money, Europe could easily service its debts and finance its imports.

Circumstances were very different when the United States imposed the Smoot-Hawley tariff. The U.S. economy was contracting and European exports to the United States had already begun to decline. American lending had been vastly curtailed, making it more difficult for Europe to service its debts. The United States' move to erect even higher trade barriers on top of that imposed in 1922 sharpened European resentment at American policy. With Smoot-Hawley, the United States seemed to be signaling that its economic policies would become more isolationist. For this reason, the European response to the passage of the Smoot-Hawley tariff "was disapproval—immediate, undisguised, and unanimous." As Percy Bidwell (1930, 130) noted: "There was a common note in the chorus of protests, however much they may have differed in expression, namely, the conviction that the new American import duties constituted a serious menace to the economic progress of western Europe."

Indeed, the tariff act came at a critical moment for the world economy. The Smoot-Hawley tariff infuriated European leaders for its bad timing. Many countries were tipping into a recession. As Congress debated Smoot-Hawley, a number of European countries were attempting to negotiate a "tariff truce" through the League of Nations. Even though the United States was not a member of the League, its action made it easier for other countries to follow suit and abandon any willingness to freeze their own tariff.

Beyond its specific economic effects, the Smoot-Hawley tariff took on a symbolic importance. To many, it seemed to represent America's indifference to the rest of the world. Charles Kindleberger (1986, 125–26, 291) does not criticize the tariff so much for economic effects, but rather for marking an abdication of U.S. economic leadership. He viewed the measure as irresponsible because it "gave rise to (or at least did nothing to stop) a headlong stampede to protection and restriction in imports, each country trying to ward off deflationary pressure of imports, and all together ensuring such pressure through mutual restriction of exports." According to Kindleberger, as well as many observers at the time, the Smoot-Hawley tariff changed the trade policy environment around the world.

Which countries were most likely to be affected by the Smoot-Hawley duties? Though it is difficult to know with any degree of precision, table 3.1 suggests that vulnerability to higher U.S. duties varied considerably. For example, although a majority of imports from Canada entered duty-free, Smoot-Hawley adversely affected almost all agricultural exports from the country. Because Cuba almost exclusively exported sugar, virtually none of its exports entered the United States duty-free and it was hit hard by higher sugar duties. Imports from Western Europe consisted mainly of manufactured goods that competed directly or indirectly with domestic production; these goods, already subject to heavy tariffs, faced even higher duties as a result of Smoot-Hawley. By contrast, many of the commodity exports of Latin American countries (such as coffee) entered the country duty-free and were unaffected by the Smoot-Hawley increase, although hides and meats from Argentina were targeted for

TABLE 3.1.
U.S. Duties on Imports by Country, 1929

	Duty-free imports (percent of total)	Average duties (percent), dutiable imports	Average duties (percent), total imports
North America			
Canada	77.3	18.1	4.0
Cuba	5.1	79.7	75.6
Mexico	73.0	27.4	7.4
Europe			
United Kingdom	49.7	35.9	17.8
France	30.6	44.6	30.8
Germany	36.8	41.5	26.0
Italy	23.6	38.9	29.5
Netherlands	31.2	48.1	32.7
Belgium	32.3	31.4	21.0
Switzerland	12.5	44.0	38.2
Sweden	79.1	27.3	5.6
Norway	48.2	29.6	15.2
Spain	34.7	34.7	22.6
Latin America			
Argentina	40.6	25.7	7.4
Brazil	97.8	57.3	1.2
Chile	97.2	33.8	0.9
Colombia	99.6	20.5	0.1
Uruguay	27.8	35.9	25.9
Venezuela	99.9	44.9	0.1
Asia			
Australia	57.9	37.5	15.7
New Zealand	54.3	36.4	16.6
India	42.1	11.9	6.9
Japan	87.4	37.1	4.5
China	72.5	39.0	10.4

Source: U.S. Tariff Commission (1931).

higher duties. Finally, Japan also managed to escape serious injury from the new tariff. Raw silk comprised about 80 percent of its exports to the United States, which was duty-free before and after Smoot-Hawley. Of course, its processed exports, such as silk fabric and chinaware, were hit by higher duties.

So what was the response of some of these countries to the Smoot-Hawley tariff?

CANADA

The U.S. and Canadian economies were highly interdependent at the time of Smoot-Hawley, as they are today. Each was the most important trading partner of the other. Of course, given the relative size of the two countries, Canada was much more dependent on the United States than vice versa. In 1929, the United States took 43 percent of Canada's exports, while Canada took 18 percent of U.S. merchandise exports. Trade was also a much larger part of Canada's economy; in 1929, exports amounted to 26 percent of its GDP. As a result, Canada was extremely sensitive about its access to the U.S. market. Because the tariff increase focused on agricultural goods that it exported, Canada was very upset with the Smoot-Hawley tariff. Not surprisingly, Canada's reaction—retaliation against U.S. exports—was probably the most significant of any foreign country and affected U.S. trade the most.

At the time that Smoot-Hawley was being considered, Canada was led by the Liberal government of Prime Minister Mackenzie King. The Liberals had traditionally pursued a pro-American foreign policy and held to a policy of tariff moderation. In fact, as late as February 1929, King was considering a reduction in Canada's tariff, but he held off because of the pending U.S. legislation (McDonald, O'Brien, and Callahan 1997). As the tariff bill worked its way through Congress, the Canadian government expressed its concern to the Hoover administration on several occasions. In November 1929, King gave a highly publicized speech in which he warned that if the United States raised tariffs on Canadian goods, Canada would respond. Indeed, the Smoot-Hawley tariff was poised to harm several segments of Canada's economy. The maritime provinces faced a doubling of the tariff on halibut and other fish, and Quebec and Ontario confronted higher duties on potatoes and dairy products. The prairie provinces were hit by the new duties on cattle and fresh meats, and British Columbia was affected by the duties on apples, logs, and lumber. Few constituencies in Canada would be exempt from the impending American tariff hike.

In early May 1930, King announced that a general election would be held in July. As it became clear around this time that Smoot-Hawley would be passed, trade policy was guaranteed to be a major issue in the campaign. This put King under domestic political pressure to respond to the U.S. action. The opposition Conservative party criticized the Liberal government for being too weak in its response to U.S. protectionism. The Conservatives wanted closer economic ties with Britain and advocated higher tariffs on American goods. In late May, to preempt the hard-line Conservative message on trade, the King government announced a reduction of duties on 270 goods imported from Britain and its dominions. Since the rates charged on American goods remained unchanged, this policy gave clear preference to dominion goods and sent the message that Canada had decided to shift its trade to Britain and expand trade within the British Empire. "Switch trade from U.S. to Britain," King wrote in his diary. "That will be the cry & it will sweep the country I believe" (Glassford 1992, 74).

In addition to the reduction of duties on British goods, the Canadian government raised its tariff to match the comparable U.S. tariff on sixteen products that represented about 30 percent of the value of U.S. exports to Canada. These were mostly agricultural goods whose producers the Smoot-Hawley tariff was supposedly designed to help, including potatoes, soups and soup preparations, livestock and meats, butter, eggs, wheat and wheat flour, oats and oatmeal, and other manufactures such as cast iron pipe. Since Canada's tariffs on those goods had been much lower than the U.S. tariff, the increase was substantial. The Canadian government did not use the term "retaliation" to describe the change, but in a campaign speech Prime Minister King said that the countervailing duties were aimed at the United States.

Still, the opposition Conservatives attacked the May response as inadequate and hoped to capitalize on the Canadian electorate's anger about the American tariff, particularly in regions that produced goods exported to the U.S. market. The protectionist, anti-American message found fertile ground. "By arousing nationalistic sentiments and contempt for the United States in Canada . . . the Smoot-Hawley Tariff provided a climate in which the [Conservatives'] ultra-protectionist rhetoric had greater appeal than the [Liberals'] endorsement of expanded imperial trade," writes Kottman (1975, 633). As a result, the Conservatives won the election. McDonald, O'Brien, and Callahan (1997) show that the election outcome was influenced by swing votes in Quebec and the prairie provinces whose exports had been particularly harmed by the Smoot-Hawley tariff.

In September 1930, the new Conservative government passed an emergency tariff that substantially increased import duties on goods such as textiles, agricultural implements, electrical equipment, meats, and many others. Most of the products came from the United States, the source of almost 70 percent of Canada's imports. Once again, officials did not use the word "retaliation" to describe the action, but the message was clear. As the *New York Times* reported: "Despite Canadian denials of reciprocal action aimed at the United States in the new Dominion tariff schedules . . . the impression appeared to be rather general tonight that Canada had made the only answer possible to the American tariff bill, and in a form which might affect an international trade situation that has already shown alarming symptoms" (September 17, 1930, 26).

What was the effect of these measures on U.S. exports to Canada? Figure 3.1 presents monthly figures for 1930 in which the effect of the May and September tariff increases can be seen in the sharp declines in U.S. exports in June–July and November–December. U.S. exports fell 15 percent in June and another 15 percent in November, followed by an 11 percent decline in December. The timing of the declines seems linked to Canada's actions, but it is difficult to know how much should be attributed to the retaliatory measure.

Another way of assessing Canada's response is to compare its imports from the United States to those from the rest of the world, as shown in figure 3.2. Through 1930, imports from the rest of the world were steady, whereas those from the United States start declining in midyear

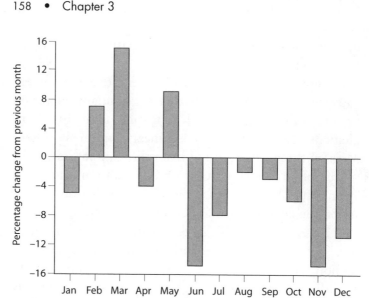

Figure 3.1. Percentage change in monthly U.S. exports to Canada, 1930. Source: Monthly Summary of Foreign Commerce of the United States, December 1930.

and nearly converge to the amount from the rest of the world.[2] If U.S. exports to Canada had maintained their proportion to rest-of-world imports, U.S. exports would have been 21 percent higher. If the difference is attributed to retaliation against the United States, then the retaliatory effect was enormous. A 21 percent reduction in U.S. exports to Canada, when those exports comprised 18 percent of total U.S. exports, implies that total U.S. exports fell by 4 percent simply as a result of Canada's response.

As chapter 2 noted, the volume of U.S. exports fell more than the volume of U.S. imports in the two years

[2] It is interesting to note that Canada's imports from the United States fell 27 percent in 1930 from the previous year, whereas its imports from Britain fell 16 percent.

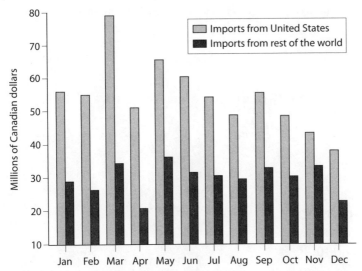

Figure 3.2. Canada's monthly imports, United States and other countries, 1930. Source: Dominion Bureau of Statistics, Quarterly Report of the Trade of Canada, 1931.

subsequent to the Smoot-Hawley tariff. If U.S. exports fell 4 percent as a result of Canada's retaliation, we can see how the Smoot-Hawley tariff could have played a large part in this decline. According to the calculations in chapter 2, the Smoot-Hawley tariff reduced total U.S. imports by about 5 percent. But if U.S. exports fell by 4 percent as a result of Canada's reaction alone, the offset to exports almost matches the entire impact of Smoot-Hawley on imports. And if other countries retaliated as well, it is easy to see why U.S. exports declined nearly as much as U.S. imports in the aftermath of Smoot-Hawley.

A simple example used by Cordell Hull, the U.S. Secretary of State from 1933 to 1944, illustrates how the Smoot-Hawley tariff backfired. The U.S. tariff on eggs rose from 8 cents to 10 cents a dozen, ostensibly to limit

Source: *Rollin Kirby Post*. Printed with permission of *Rollin Kirby Post*.

Right Back at Us!
—Talburt in the Washington "Daily News."

Source: *Washington Daily News*

imports and boost domestic egg prices for farmers. Canada was so incensed that, as previously noted, they raised their own tariff on certain products to match the new U.S. tariff. In this case, they increased their tariff on imported eggs from 3 cents to 10 cents a dozen. While American imports of eggs from Canada fell from 13,299 dozen in 1929 to 7,939 dozen in 1932, American exports of eggs to Canada dropped from 919,543 dozen to 13,662 dozen over the same period (Hull 1948, 1: 355).

CUBA

The Smoot-Hawley tariff had a devastating impact on another neighboring country, Cuba. The Cuban economy was enormously dependent upon exports of sugar to the United States. The increase in the sugar duty was a major blow to the Cuban economy.

Dye and Sicotte (2003) estimate that one-third to one-half of the decline in Cuba's export earnings after 1930 was caused by the passage of the Smoot-Hawley tariff. According to their calculations, the U.S. sugar tariff erased 10 percent of Cuba's national income between 1929 and 1933, amounting to more than a third of the overall decline in Cuba's GDP over that period. By reducing Cuba's national income, the Smoot-Hawley tariff reduced Cuban demand for imports from the United States. Although less than 3 percent of total U.S. exports were sent to Cuba, the direct damage to these exports as a result of the tariff is evident.

Of course, the Great Depression would have caused Cuba's economic conditions to deteriorate even without Smoot-Hawley. But the tariff clearly contributed to Cuba's severe economic problems and also to the overthrow of the pro-American government in the revolution of 1933. The revolution fundamentally changed Cuban politics and the country's economic policies, and represented a repudiation of the United States. "This sentiment among the Cuban people is not difficult to explain," Dye and Sicotte (2003) note. "One of the strongest trading partners with the United States, and perhaps the strongest ally, in the western hemisphere before 1933, Cubans afterward developed a strong sense of having been betrayed and abused."[3]

WESTERN EUROPE

As already noted, Western Europe reacted with visceral hostility to the higher American duties. The European press and public opinion, industry and agriculture, and government officials were all appalled by the action. Here was the world's largest creditor nation, with a substantial trade surplus, restricting the trade of countries that were trying to pay off their burdensome World War I debts. Here was a country that had spurned the League of Nations, now undermining the League's efforts to negotiate a multilateral tariff truce. Here was the world's leading economic power—a country that had enjoyed robust economic growth through the 1920s while Europe struggled with postwar reconstruction—significantly increasing its import tariffs after having already done so in 1922.

Of course the tariff was a diplomatic affront, but only 6 percent of the continent's exports were destined for the

[3] Dye and Sicotte (2004) similarly show that the tightening of the U.S. sugar quota for Cuba in 1956 played a role in bringing about the 1959 communist revolution there.

U.S. market. So why did the U.S. action provoke such intense bitterness and resentment in Europe?[4] The answer lies in the importance and nature of Europe's exports. Those exports were critical in earning scarce dollars to pay debts and finance imports. And the exports consisted of highly specialized manufactured goods in key industries. Because U.S. manufacturers were so efficient at mass production and high tariffs protected American-made goods, European exporters faced significant obstacles in selling in the United States. Only European producers of high-priced specialty goods could overcome the high import duties and find a market. Yet the Smoot-Hawley tariff was designed to squeeze out even these goods, which were minor from the standpoint of the U.S. economy but critical for European manufacturers. As Jones (1934, 16) put it, when the Smoot-Hawley tariff "can threaten with ruin these specialized industries in foreign countries, when it can arouse the population of Switzerland through an increased duty on watches, when it can arouse the French nation through a proposed increase in the duty on a particular kind of lace, when it can arouse bitterness through Spain by an increased duty on cork, throughout Italy by an increased duty on olive oil, throughout Canada by increased duties upon a negligible flow of borderline traffic in foodstuffs and raw products— then our tariff assumes

[4] Bidwell (1930) provides a good contemporary analysis of the reasons for Europe's particularly hostile reaction. As he puts it, European attitudes "can be understood only by reference to American commercial policy and our economic relations with Europe during the past eight or ten years. While the United States has strengthened its position year by year as the leading economic and financial power of the world, Europe has wrestled with only indifferent success with the problems of recovery from the war. One of the fundamental conditions for recovery is the development of export markets outside of Europe."

in the eyes of foreigners the features of discrimination in fact, if not in form."[5]

For many countries, the possibilities for retaliation were limited by a most-favored nation (MFN) agreement with the United States. An MFN agreement meant they could not discriminate in their tariff schedule against the United States, and vice versa.[6] The Smoot-Hawley increase did not violate MFN agreements because it was non-discriminatory; it applied to imports from all countries. A country undertaking retaliation against it would have to increase its tariffs against all its other trading partners as well, which most countries did not want to do.

Yet there were many ways of getting around the formal requirement that tariffs be imposed in a non-discriminatory fashion. Duties could be increased selectively on products that came largely from the United States, such as automobiles, razor blades, and sewing machines. Trade restrictions imposed on grounds of health and safety did not need to meet the requirement of non-discrimination. This provision opened the door for many quiet but implicit retaliations. For example, just three days after the

[5] "It is difficult for Americans to appreciate the vital necessity of export markets to the manufacturers of such nations as England, Germany, Belgium, Switzerland, and Austria," Bidwell (1930, 14–15) wrote. "Consider, then, the importance which must be attributed in Germany to export markets which absorb 25 percent of its silk goods, and equal proportion of its rolling mill products and from 50 to 60 percent of its metal wares; or in Belgium, which exports 90 percent of its plate glass and window glass and 60 percent of its cement; or in Switzerland, which exports 95 percent of its production of watches and 98 percent of its embroideries."

[6] There were exceptions. In the MFN agreements, other countries always reserved the right to exchange tariff preferences with their colonies, just as the United States was allowed to give preferential treatment to imports from the Philippines and Cuba.

passage of the Smoot-Hawley tariff, Britain prohibited the importation of certain apples from the United States supposedly for reasons of sanitation and public health. Argentina restricted imports of American eggs, ostensibly for the same reasons. Import quotas were also exempt from the non-discrimination requirement, so countries could always limit the allocation given to U.S. goods.

Most Western European countries looked to France to organize a unified response to the American tariff. The French press was outraged by the Smoot-Hawley tariff, and the French Chamber of Deputies urged retaliation and the withdrawal of MFN treatment for U.S. goods. In April 1930, France imposed higher taxes on imported automobiles, to take effect in June. Although the action was not announced as a response to Smoot-Hawley, singling out automobiles—a product uniquely identified with the United States—seems indicative of implicit retaliation.

Officially, the French government took a cautious approach that quieted demands for a full-scale European response. The French Minister of Commerce, Pierre Flandin, indicated that France would conduct a thorough survey of the impact of the new American tariff on French exports. Once the review was completed, France planned to ask the Hoover administration to use the flexible tariff provision to reduce excessive rates on French exports. "If we succeed in obtaining a revision of certain new duties bearing heavily on our export trade, there will be no reason for seeking to poison our relations with a country which had rendered us measurable assistance in the World War," Flandin stated. "Nevertheless, should the Tariff Commission refuse seriously to consider our protests, we must then frankly face the problem and proceed with other measures. . . . Just what measures could be taken remains undetermined, but it is very clear that normal commercial relations between the various countries cannot be assured except by application of the principle of strict reciprocity" (*New York Times*, June 22, 1930, 1).

In fact, the French review never amounted to much and the issue may have been dropped. Instead, France focused on tariff negotiations within Europe and implementation of a new French commercial policy. In mid-1931, France began to use more import quotas, which were not subject to MFN rules. With quotas, it was much easier to discriminate against certain suppliers, such as the United States.

Germany also refrained from explicitly retaliating against the United States. German public opinion was dismayed by the new tariff (a "monster of economic folly," according to the *Frankfurter Zeitung*), but the government made no official response. However, German officials were upset with the action because it made it even more difficult for the country to earn the dollars necessary to pay its reparations from World War I. Like France, they put their hope in President Hoover's ability to use the flexible tariff provision to reduce excessive duties.

Britain also did not respond formally to the Smoot-Hawley duties. In that country, "ministers resisted pressure to join in the protest on account of [Prime Minister Ramsay] MacDonald's initiative to improve Anglo-American relations" (Boyce 2009, 264). However, as will be discussed, its commercial policy changed dramatically within two years of the Smoot-Hawley tariff.

Several other smaller European countries were more direct about taking action against the United States in response to Smoot-Hawley. These include Spain, Italy,

Switzerland, and Portugal (Jones 1934). Spain, which had
long-simmering trade disputes with the United States
and France, announced the Wais tariff on July 22, 1930.
This act significantly raised duties imposed on imported
automobiles. It added a provision particularly aimed at
U.S. automobiles—an extra duty on non-European cars
assembled in Europe and shipped to Spain. As a result,
U.S. car exports to Spain dropped by 94 percent in three
years, while British, German, and Canadian cars were
unaffected by the duties and saw their sales surge (Jones
1934, 53).

The Wais tariff also increased duties on sewing machines, razor blades, tires and tubes, and motion pictures,
products typically imported from the United States. U.S.
exports to Spain fell 54 percent in September 1930, likely
the result of the new tariff, but they bounced back later in
the year. Spain also withdrew most-favored nation treatment from the United States so that Spain was free to
discriminate against American commerce. Despite these
measures, evidence of undue discrimination against U.S.
exports is not readily apparent; the U.S. share of Spain's
imports in 1935 was the same as it had been in 1928.

In Italy, Benito Mussolini threatened the United States
with retaliatory action. On June 30, 1930, just days after
Smoot-Hawley took effect, Italy more than doubled the
import tariff imposed on foreign automobiles. The tax
was not officially called retaliation for the Smoot-Hawley
tariff, but most press accounts viewed it as such, particularly because about 80 percent of Italy's automobile imports came from the United States. In September, higher
duties were imposed on radios and radio equipment,
products that also came largely from the United States. In
addition, the Italian government had some control over

the country's purchases of bulk commodities and used its influence to shift its source of cotton, wheat, copper, and other goods from the United States. For example, Italian imports of wheat from the United States fell in 1931, while they rose from Russia. Overall, the U.S. share of Italy's imports fell from 18 percent in 1929 to 11 percent in 1935, consistent with increased discrimination against U.S. goods.

Switzerland was extremely hard hit by the higher duties on imported watches in the Smoot-Hawley tariff. About 20 percent of its watch production was exported to the United States, and the tariff had a devastating effect on Swiss exports. U.S. imports from Switzerland dropped from a monthly average of $3.2 million (February–April 1930) to $1.7 million (July–September 1930), a decline of 48 percent. Switzerland recognized that retaliation against the United States would accomplish nothing. But the outrage of Swiss public opinion led to an informal boycott, encouraged by the Chamber of Commerce, aimed at slashing sales of American-made automobiles, typewriters, and other goods. It is difficult to know how much of an impact the boycott had, but Switzerland's imports from the United States fell almost 30 percent in 1930, whereas its total imports fell by just 5 percent (Jones 1934, 122). In the early 1930s, Switzerland also began imposing import quotas, which could be administered in a way to shift imports between suppliers. The portion of Switzerland's imports from the United States fell from 9 percent in 1928 to 6 percent in 1935—a loss of market share that is consistent with discrimination against U.S. goods.

Finally, Portugal's government announced that it would retaliate against the United States by imposing the Smoot-Hawley duties on its imports from the United States. Whether this plan ever took effect is unclear.

In sum, unlike Canada, European countries generally refrained from a direct retaliatory response to the Smoot-Hawley tariff. Although some smaller countries did respond, the effect on total U.S. exports was probably slight. Still, the fears of Henry Ford and Alfred Sloan were correct: the automobile was judged to be the quintessential American product and hence it was targeted for retribution. But if formal acts of retaliation were relatively few, it seems that subtle retaliation did come in the form of discrimination against U.S. commerce.

PROTECTIONISM AND DISCRIMINATION

The United States was the first major country to increase its tariff at the start of the Depression. It seemed to trigger a wave of tariff increases in other countries. As the League of Nations (1933, 193) put it at the time: "The Hawley-Smoot tariff in the United States was the signal for an outburst of tariff-making activity in other countries, partly least by way of reprisals. Extensive increases in duties were made almost immediately by Canada, Cuba, Mexico, France, Italy, [and] Spain."[7] As protectionist trade policies spread throughout the world, world trade experienced a sharp decline.[8] Was the Smoot-Hawley tariff responsible

[7] Observing the wave of tariff revisions that followed Smoot-Hawley, the League of Nations (1931, 4) did remark: "It would be wrong to assert that these revisions were meant as reprisals, but it is, nevertheless, true that they raised the duties on characteristic exports of the United States."

[8] The volume of world trade fell 26 percent between 1929 and 1932 (League of Nations 1933, 45). According to one study, 42 percent of this decline was due to lower income and 58 percent was due to higher tariff and non-tariff barriers (Madsen 2001b).

for the outbreak of protectionism and the collapse in trade during the early 1930s?

World trade relations clearly deteriorated between 1930 and mid-1931, the period immediately following Smoot-Hawley. However, this is largely because some countries were reacting to the spread of the Depression and imposing higher tariffs, particularly on specific agricultural goods; it was not necessarily a reaction to Smoot-Hawley and probably would have occurred even if Congress had not passed the bill. But this initial movement toward higher trade barriers only disrupted the world trading system; it did not destroy it. Indeed, reviewing trade policy developments between September 1929 and March 1931, a League of Nations (1931) report lamented the fact that tariffs were rising around the world, but it was not alarmist and did not claim that the developments were catastrophic for world trade.

While protectionism did ultimately undermine the world trading system, the trade barriers arose not so much in response to Smoot-Hawley as to a financial crisis that spread throughout Europe in the summer of 1931.[9] A banking crisis in Austria led to a financial panic and currency crisis that spread to neighboring countries. Facing a rapid loss of its gold and foreign exchange reserves, Germany and Hungary imposed restrictive controls on foreign exchange transactions that impeded trade and capital flows alike. Exchange controls mean that all foreign exchange is controlled and allocated by the government. Governments used exchange controls not only to prevent capital flight, but also to reduce spending on imports. As such, they were among the most restrictive trade practices of the 1930s.

[9] This section draws on Eichengreen and Irwin (2010).

By August, financial pressure had spread to Britain. Following attempts to support the pound on foreign exchange markets, Britain abandoned the gold standard in September 1931 and allowed the pound to depreciate against other currencies on foreign exchange markets. The depreciation of the pound meant that British exports were now more price-competitive on world markets, while imports were more expensive. Other countries whose currency was tied to the pound sterling, including Denmark, Norway, and Sweden, also allowed their currencies to depreciate.

Even though there were sound economic reasons for Britain's action, it unfortunately led to a breakdown of international trade relations. The British move triggered a defensive response by countries that remained on the gold standard. It put other countries under financial pressure and forced them to impose exchange controls to prevent capital outflows. In September–October 1931, many countries implemented exchange controls, among them: Uruguay, Colombia, Greece, Czechoslovakia, Iceland, Bolivia, Yugoslavia, Austria, Argentina, Belgium, Norway, and Denmark. Others responded to the devaluation by imposing higher trade barriers against countries whose currency had depreciated on foreign exchange markets. A month after the British devaluation, France imposed a 15 percent surcharge on British goods to offset the depreciation of sterling and shifted toward greater use of import quotas. By 1936, nearly two-thirds of French imports were restricted by such quotas. In early 1932, the Netherlands, which traditionally had a policy of free trade, increased duties by 25 percent, partly to offset the competitive advantage gained by sterling area producers.

The collapse of the gold standard in September 1931 wrought much greater havoc to world trade than the Smoot-Hawley tariff had in June 1930. As the League of Nations (1933, 16–17) reported:

> In the sixteen months after September 1, 1931, general tariff increases had been imposed in twenty-three countries, in three of them twice during the period—with only one case of a general tariff reduction. Customs duties had been increased on individual items or groups of commodities by fifty countries.... Import quotas, prohibitions, licensing systems and similar quantitative restrictions, with even more frequent changes in several important cases, had been imposed by thirty-two countries.... This bare list is utterly inadequate to portray the harassing complexity of the emergency restrictions that were superimposed upon an already fettered world trade after the period of exchange instability was inaugurated by the abandonment of the gold standard by the United Kingdom in September 1931. By the middle of 1932, it was obvious that the international trading mechanism was in real danger of being smashed as completely as the international monetary system had.

To compound the problems that followed from the depreciation of the pound, Britain also changed its trade policy. It abandoned its long-standing policy of free trade and now moved toward a policy of protectionism. A month after Britain left the gold standard, a general election returned a National Government dominated by the Conservative party, which had traditionally favored using tariffs to help domestic industries. In November 1931, the new parliament enacted the Abnormal Importations Act, which gave the Board of Trade administrative discretion to increase tariffs by up to 100 percent on goods as it deemed fit. In February 1932, parliament approved the Import Duties Act of 1932, which imposed a general tariff of 10 percent on most imports. This marked an end to Britain's long-standing policy of free and nondiscriminatory trade. Whereas 70 percent of U.S. exports entered Britain duty-free in 1930, by the end of the next year, only 20 percent did (Jones 1934, 238).

As other countries sank deeper into recession, they attempted to stimulate their economies by imposing more restrictions on imports. One country might be able to get away with reducing its imports and still selling its exports, providing some boost to the economy. But if every country tried to insulate itself from the effects of the depression via increased trade barriers, the end result would be a decline in every country's imports and exports. Because a reduction in one country's imports amounted to a reduction in another country's exports, higher trade barriers became known as "beggar thy neighbor" policy. The end result was a destruction of trade in which no one was better off.

If the United States had not enacted the Smoot-Hawley tariff, protectionist trade policies still would have proliferated as a consequence of the world's economic and financial turmoil in 1931. And world trade still would have fallen sharply with the deepening of the depression. Thus, the Smoot-Hawley tariff was just one of many factors that contributed to the protectionism of the early 1930s. Sir

Hands Across the Sea!

—Talburt in the Washington "Daily News."

Source: *Washington Daily News*

Arthur Salter, the British civil servant who wrote in 1932 that Smoot-Hawley marked "a turning point in world history," later revised his view. "It seemed at the time a wanton blow at the world's hopes for a more stable foundation for the expansion of international trade and general increase of prosperity," Salter (1961, 198) recalled. "A little later it was seen to be only a significant reflection of much more powerful disruptive forces."

Yet this interpretation does little to exonerate it. While it may have played a limited role in the spread of protectionism and the collapse of world trade in the early 1930s, the Smoot-Hawley tariff helped give rise to an especially damaging development: the spread of discriminatory trade policies. And because of the smoldering resentment of the American tariff, the United States was a particular target of those discriminatory policies.

Discriminatory trade policies shift trade flows between countries to a much greater extent than non-discriminatory trade policies. If a foreign country increased its tariffs on all imports, U.S. exports would likely decline in the same proportion as other exports to that market; in other words, the United States would maintain its share of a smaller market. However, if there is even a slight amount of discrimination against American goods that resulted in favoring other suppliers, it could shift the entire market against the United States.

The most damaging discriminatory measure affecting U.S. trade at this time was the imperial preferences created by Britain and her former colonies in 1932. In essence, Britain helped establish tariff preferences to encourage trade among its dominions, principally Australia, Canada, New Zealand, and South Africa, as well as colonies that had tariff autonomy, such as India. These coun-

The Builder Spoils the Architect's Plans
—"Irish Weekly Independent" (Dublin).

Source: *The Independent* (Ireland). Reprinted with permission from Independent Newspapers (Ireland).

tries had long sought preferential access in Britain for their exports of agricultural goods and raw materials and in exchange offered preferences for British manufactures in their market in exchange. Since the mid-nineteenth century, Britain maintained a policy of non-discriminatory free trade and did not offer tariff preferences. But the Conservative-dominated government elected in October 1931 was much more supportive of closer economic ties with the dominions than the Liberal or Labour party, both of whom opposed any retreat from free trade. In early 1932, the government imposed a 10 percent general tariff, with an exception for products of the Empire. This positioned the country to implement imperial preferences.

At a conference in Ottawa in July–August 1932, at the instigation of Canada's Conservative government, Britain agreed to a formal system of imperial preferences. The Canadian government, as we have seen, was motivated by a desire to shift its trade away from the United States toward Britain. And therefore Smoot-Hawley played an indirect role in bringing this about. Indeed, the Conservative prime minister defended the Ottawa agreements before parliament by stating that the country needed an advantage over the United States in exporting its goods to the United Kingdom to make up for the lost U.S. markets as a result of the Smoot-Hawley tariff. "Unquestionably the American Congress had precipitated the tariff responses in both Canada and the United Kingdom," Kottman (1968, 37) argues. "Shortly before the Ottawa Conference, the American chargé in the Canadian capital reported a 'quiet but definite undercurrent of antagonism and bitterness towards the United States trade policy' whenever comments were made of the impending gathering." Furthermore, this official noted, "most of the people I have talked to have not failed to refer to our tariff and to accuse it of starting the world movement toward restriction of trade."[10]

How much did imperial preferences harm U.S. export interests? Initial impressions by exporters suggested that

[10] In discussing the international ramifications of the Smoot-Hawley tariff, the League of Nations (1931, 4) stated that "it would also appear that the American tariffs have given a stimulus to the movement for a more extended and more pronounced system of Customs preferences within the British Empire."

AN INTERESTED LISTENER-IN
From the Montreal *Star*

This Canadian newspaper calls the Dominion Conference a business
gathering, with Uncle Sam perhaps a little worried.

Source: *Montreal Star*.

between $75 million and $200 million of U.S. exports would get diverted as a result of the Ottawa agreements, amounting to 5–13 percent of U.S. exports in 1931 (*New York Times*, August 28, 1932, F9). Even taking the lower figure, this is a very large impact. Secretary of State Cordell Hull later contended that "the greatest injury, in a commercial way, that has been inflicted on this country since I have been in public life was the great increase in the British Empire preference that followed the Smoot-Hawley tariff. That was an act of direct retaliation" (Irwin, Mavroidis, and Sykes 2008, 10). Imperial preferences put U.S. exporters at a significant cost disadvantage; by 1937, about half of British exports to and imports from the Commonwealth enjoyed, on average, preferences on the order of 20 percent (Macdougall and Hutt 1954). It was difficult for U.S. exporters to compete in these markets when their competitors had such an advantage.

Discrimination had a pronounced effect on U.S. exports to two of its largest markets, Canada and Britain, which together took about a third of U.S. exports in 1929. As table 3.2 shows, the U.S. share of Canada's imports fell significantly in the early 1930s, as did its share of Britain's imports.[11]

Furthermore, it was not just Britain and her allies that shunned trade with the United States. In 1931, Germany began using a host of discriminatory trade instruments, ranging from exchange controls, import licensing, and bilateral clearing arrangements with countries in south

[11] A later idiosyncratic study suggested no great injury overall because U.S. exports to the British market did not compete much with British imports from its Empire partners, but important adverse effects on exports of bacon, tobacco, timber, and fruit to Britain, prunes, textiles, and chemicals to Canada, timber to Australia, and automobiles to New Zealand (Glickman 1947, 468).

TABLE 3.2.
U.S. Share of Imports, Canada and United Kingdom

Share of imports into	1929 (percent)	1933 (percent)
Canada		
From United States	69	54
From United Kingdom	15	24
United Kingdom		
From United States	16	11
From British Empire	29	39

Source: Hart (2002, 96); Kottman (1968, 117).

eastern Europe. Germany's imports from the United States fell from 15 percent of total imports in 1928 to 6 percent in 1935. Similarly, France began using discriminatory import quotas to regulate its trade, and its imports from the United States fell from 12 percent to 9 percent of total imports between 1928 and 1935 (League of Nations 1942).

Figure 3.3 shows the impact on U.S. foreign trade. While the fall in world imports corresponded to the fall in world industrial production between 1929 and 1932, imports from the United States declined by a much greater extent. World imports fell 25 percent from 1929 to 1932, while imports from the United States fell 49 percent. The U.S. share of world exports fell from 15.6 percent in 1929 to 12.4 percent in 1932, according to the League of Nations. The United States was cut out of a substantial part of world trade during the 1930s, representing a significant loss of commercial opportunities. This helps explain why

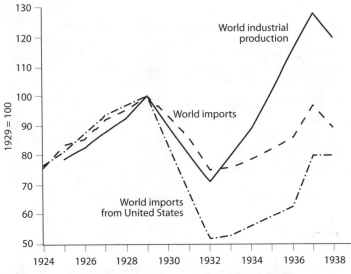

Figure 3.3. World imports and imports from the United States, 1925–1939. Source: Lary (1943, 8).

real net exports were a drag on U.S. economic growth until after 1936, as chapter 2 showed.

In sum, the international economic environment in 1932 was dramatically different from what it had been in 1929. The United States bears some of the responsibility for what unfolded. What was the U.S. response to these developments at the time? The Hoover administration essentially had no plan. The president blamed the Depression on Europe and insisted that, because of the deepening slump, high import duties were even more critical to protecting the American economy. Republicans in Congress were unrepentant at having enacted the tariff of 1930. They insisted that it had prevented the Depression from being even worse. And so nothing was done.

Conclusion

One of the many controversial questions surrounding the Smoot-Hawley tariff is the degree to which it was responsible for the world's slide to protectionism in the 1930s. Undoubtedly, because of the Depression, many countries would have erected trade barriers even if the Smoot-Hawley tariff had never been implemented. But although Smoot-Hawley was not entirely responsible for the massive outbreak of protectionism in the early 1930s, it certainly contributed to the climate in which such policies flourished.

Smoot-Hawley clearly inspired retaliatory moves against the United States, particularly—but not exclusively—by Canada. This retaliation had a significant effect in reducing U.S. exports. Even worse, Smoot-Hawley generated ill-will around the world and led to widespread discrimination against U.S. exports. Because discriminatory measures affect trade flows across countries more than non-discriminatory measures, U.S. exports were severely affected by them, and America's share of world trade fell sharply in the early 1930s. Having helped poison international trade relations, the United States would spend the better part of the next two decades trying to dismantle the discriminatory trade blocs that had put U.S. exporters at such a significant disadvantage in major foreign markets.

Chapter 4

Aftermath and Legacy

THE DEBATE OVER the Smoot-Hawley tariff did not end in June 1930. Leading newspapers, Congressional Democrats, business leaders, and economists continued to criticize it long after its passage. In widely reported comments at a November 1930 conference, Thomas W. Lamont (1931, 92–93) complained that:

> we have complicated this situation of ours . . . by hanging the load of a new tariff act around our own necks. The increased rates have certainly led to a certain feeling of dismay and ill-will abroad and to some retaliatory tariffs. They have probably also caused some harm both to home trade and to our international commerce, because of the uncertainties and dislocations which they have created. It would be easy to magnify the ill results of the new

American tariff. We cannot class them as controlling factors in our present depression. But there can be little dispute that we chose a most inopportune time for this particular tariff enactment. With both domestic and foreign trade beginning to show signs of a decline, as they did in the early summer of 1929, it surely was not the time to build up new barriers against world trade.

Reed Smoot immediately responded to Lamont's remarks:

I have little patience with statements that the new tariff is retarding business recuperation. Thousands and thousands of people are at work today with the boot and shoe and textile and other industries who would be idle except for the new tariff. The prices of corn, butter, wool and other agricultural products are higher today than they would have been, as is proved by the prices everywhere else in the world . . . Far from reprisals as the result of our increased tariff, only one nation has increased its tariffs since we undertook revision, and that hardly affects us at all.

Smoot concluded that, with the gap between American and foreign wages widening, "the question is now whether the tariff is high enough, not whether it is too high" (*New York Times*, November 16, 1930, 1).

In a prominent article published in 1932, Harvard economist Sumner Slichter (1932, 522) called the Smoot-

Hawley tariff "an act of almost incredible economic folly" and expressed his belief that it was "a major influence in making the world vulnerable to depression and in intensifying the slump when it came." Smoot utterly rejected this view, arguing that the Depression would have been much worse without the higher tariff. He insisted that countries were not retaliating against Smoot-Hawley but simply acting in their own interest. "In this hour of national distress protection is imperative," Smoot (1931) stated. Without the 1930 tariff increase, "America would have become a dumping ground for all the surplus products of the world." "The Smoot-Hawley tariff has proved to be a shock absorber against world-wide dumping. . . . Jobs are now far more important than cheap goods." And he denied that the United States started the move toward higher tariffs:

> It is difficult to understand why any one should try to fasten responsibility for the general movement toward higher protective duties upon the United States. Many nations revised their tariffs before Congress passed the Smoot-Hawley bill in June 1930, and many have increased their duties since. Each country has been prompted by economic considerations of its own. . . . Only the purblind egotist can suggest that the world turned to protection in retaliation against the American tariff.

Smoot was completely convinced that the tariff legislation bearing his name had aided the economy. As his biographer put it:

HOPING THE PEOPLE HAVE FORGOTTEN

Source: *St. Louis Post-Dispatch* Editorial Cartoon Collection. Courtesy of the State Historical Society of Missouri.

In the Senate, on the stump, in the magazines, through the press, he replied methodically to the attacks. There is no suggestion in any speech or letter of his after the act was passed that he had the slightest tremor of doubt about its wisdom or beneficence. Rarely did he make a speech—and he delivered dozens of them—without the inclusion of a defense of Smoot-Hawley, either against specific charges or in general terms. (Merrill 1990, 338)

Some economists feared that Smoot-Hawley might get a good reputation if the economy began to turn around in 1931. As noted in chapter 2, many previous tariff acts had been enacted near the trough of a business cycle, allowing proponents to claim that higher tariffs were responsible for the subsequent economic recovery. As Frank Taussig (1930, 19) cautioned:

[I]t is possible that in future days the [Smoot-Hawley] act will come to be glorified as having rescued the entire country from disaster. The present period of depression will run its course; in one year or two or three—who can say how soon?—matters will once more be moving smoothly and prosperously. Then the chronology and meaning of the events of 1929–30 will be forgotten by most people, and it will be possible to say that there was a great panic in 1929, and that the sovereign remedy was applied in the Tariff Act of 1930 and promptly brought a return to prosperity. Stranger talk is a familiar

YESTERDAY'S PROPHETS.

Source: *St. Louis Post-Dispatch* Editorial Cartoon Collection. Courtesy of the State Historical Society of Missouri.

part of our tariff debates, nor is there any clear indication that it fails to serve the protection-ist's turn.

However, this pattern did not repeat itself. The recovery was not just around the corner after the passage of the Smoot-Hawley tariff; instead, the economy deteriorated even further in 1931 and 1932 and world trade continued to fall.

Despite the continued economic decline, Smoot and Hawley were unrepentant about their role in the tariff that bore their name. Unfortunately for them, as the Depression intensified and trade barriers proliferated, the reputation of the Smoot-Hawley tariff—never very positive—deteriorated even further. The sequence of events in the early 1930s accounts for the common perception at the time that the Smoot-Hawley tariff was partly responsible for the spread of protectionism around the world. It is not surprising that many believed that it helped aggravate the economic catastrophe of the period.

The unfolding economic disaster invigorated the low-tariff wing of the Democratic Party that had been dormant during much of the 1920s. The poor state of the economy allowed the Democrats to capture control of the House of Representatives in the mid-term election of 1930. In August 1931, Sen. Kenneth McKellar (D-TN) proposed to repeal the Smoot-Hawley tariff and enact an immediate, across-the-board tariff cut of 25 percent. Although most Democrats thought that Smoot-Hawley was unwise, this idea was a political non-starter. With unemployment still rising and foreign trade barriers against U.S. exports proliferating, even the Democrats could not muster any political support for a unilateral tariff reduction.[1]

Instead, Democrats and progressive Republicans joined forces to draft legislation that would take the "flexible tariff" authority away from the president and give it back to Congress, as well as create an office of consumers' council at the Tariff Commission. They also wanted to encourage the president to confer with other countries to foster friendlier trade relations, although without giving him specific authorization to reduce tariffs. "There is a widespread belief among the people of the United States that by reason of the high and exorbitant rates of the tariff act of 1930 we have incurred the hostility of many nations throughout the world," the Ways and Means Committee reported. "They believe that this hostility has resulted in the enactment of many retaliatory tariffs against us, the results of which are causing uneasiness and concern to all thoughtful minds" (House Report No. 29, 72d Congress, 1st Session).

[1] The Democrats also demonstrated that they were not immune to the logrolling that led to higher tariffs by slipping several higher tariffs into the Revenue Act of 1932. The House included higher tariffs on oil and coal in the bill, and the Senate Finance Committee fought a close, bitter fight over whether such protective duties deserved inclusion in a revenue measure. Robert LaFollette lost by a single vote a motion to restrict the bill to revenue measures only. After several votes on the tariffs, copper and lumber were added to a list of goods with increased duties. This was followed by motions to add vegetable oil, butter, manganese-bearing ores, and an export debenture for agricultural goods. With the political process threatening to spin out of control with logrolling once again, this time in Democratic hands, the Senate leadership managed to reject these additional amendments. The additional tariffs for oil, coal, copper, and lumber interests all received support from Democrats, putting Reed Smoot in the position of disavowing his party's responsibility for the action. President Hoover signed the bill, but the episode revealed that Congressional Democrats were little better than their Republican counterparts in being able to resist the pressures from certain powerful local interests.

In early 1932, the House and Senate passed this bill in highly partisan votes. Not surprisingly, President Hoover promptly vetoed it. In his veto message, Hoover (1976, 205–7) objected to the elimination of presidential authority over the flexible tariff, arguing that the provision was "the proper way to eliminate excessive duties and any injustices in the tariff and to provide flexibility to changed economic conditions." Hoover argued that "there never has been a time in the history of the United States when tariff protection was more essential to the welfare of the American people than at present" because of lower foreign prices, due in part to the depreciation of foreign currencies. "Under such conditions it is imperative that the American protective policy be maintained."

Hoover also dismissed the call for international negotiations, arguing that the tariff was "solely a domestic question." He worried that such a conference "would surrender our own control of an important part of our domestic affairs to the influence of other nations or alternatively would lead us into futilities in international negotiations." Instead, he offered this challenge: "if the Congress proposes to make such a radical change in our historic policies by international negotiation affecting the whole of American tariffs, then it is the duty of the Congress to state so frankly and indicate the extent to which it is prepared to go."

Toward a New Trade Policy

The presidential election of 1932 hinged on the Hoover administration's handling of the economy. With the economy still in the grips of the Great Depression, the political fortune of incumbent Republicans was grim. Both

Smoot and Hawley lost their seats in the 1932 election; Smoot lost to his Democratic opponent, while Hawley failed even to win the Republican primary. Yet it is doubtful that their role in crafting the 1930 tariff was directly responsible for bringing their congressional careers to an end; almost all Republicans had difficulty getting reelected in 1932.

In their election platform, the Republicans were unapologetic for having enacted the Smoot-Hawley tariff. The party declared that it "has always been the staunch supporter of the American system of a protective tariff. . . . No pretext can justify the surrender of that market to such competition as would destroy our farms, mines and factories, and lower the standard of living which we have established for our workers. . . . adequate tariff protection is today particularly essential to the welfare of the American people" (Porter and Johnson 1956, 343). Meanwhile, the Democratic platform read: "We condemn the Hawley-Smoot Tariff Law, the prohibitive rates of which have resulted in retaliatory action by more than forty countries, created international economic hostility, destroyed international trade, driven our factories into foreign countries, robbed the American farmer of his foreign markets, and increased the cost of production" (Porter and Johnson 1956, 333).

As expected, the Democrats swept into office in a landslide. This gave President Franklin Roosevelt and the Democratic Congress an opportunity to reshape U.S. trade policy. During the campaign, Roosevelt had sharply criticized the Smoot-Hawley tariff, calling it the Grundy tariff for its association with lobbyists. But with the unemployment rate so high, he was reluctant to call for any tariff reductions. Instead, he and his secretary of state,

Cordell Hull, decided to undertake negotiations with other countries to reduce tariffs at home and abroad. In 1934, they proposed the Reciprocal Trade Agreements Act (RTAA) in which Congress would delegate to the president the power to adjust import duties up or down as much as 50 percent in such trade agreements. In his message to Congress requesting the authority, President Roosevelt explicitly noted the discrimination that the United States faced in world markets:

> Other Governments are to an ever-increasing extent winning their share of international trade by negotiated reciprocal trade agreements. If American agricultural and industrial interests are to retain their deserved place in this trade, the American Government must be in a position to bargain for that place with other Governments by rapid and decisive negotiation based upon a carefully considered program, and to grant with discernment corresponding opportunities in the American market for foreign products supplementary to our own. If the American Government is not in a position to make fair offers for fair opportunities, its trade will be superseded. If it is not in a position at a given moment rapidly to alter the terms on which it is willing to deal with other countries, it cannot adequately protect its trade against discriminations and against bargains injurious to its interests. (*Congressional Record*, March 2, 1934, 3580)

The Democratic Congress quickly and overwhelmingly passed the RTAA. In his memoirs, Hull (1948, 1:

357) argued that "in both House and Senate we were aided by the severe reaction of public opinion against the Smoot-Hawley Act." In fact, the RTAA's passage did not reflect a general repudiation of Smoot-Hawley by Congress or a change in the underlying tariff preferences of individual members. Instead, the change is explained simply by the massive shift in the partisan composition of Congress, with low-tariff Democrats replacing high-tariff Republicans. After examining the votes of all members of Congress who voted on both the Smoot-Hawley bill and the RTAA, Schnietz (2000) clearly demonstrates that Congress did not "change its mind" about the wisdom of the measure. That would imply that members who voted for Smoot-Hawley later regretted it and voted for the RTAA. Of the ninety-five members of Congress who voted in favor of Smoot-Hawley, only nine voted in favor of the RTAA. Of those nine, seven were Democrats; only two of eighty-six Republicans changed their view.

One of them, Sen. Arthur Capper from Kansas, may have changed his mind due to the series of unfortunate events that followed the passage of Smoot-Hawley.[2] As Capper stated:

> I am a firm believer in the protective tariff. But it has seemed to me ever since we enacted the latest tariff act . . . that the United States has a Gordian knot to undo in the matter of interference with world trade by tariffs, quotas, embargos, and similar trade restrictions. I do not

[2] The other was Sen. James Couzens of Michigan, who did not make a statement in the *Congressional Record* about his change in view, but who had become a "New Deal" Republican.

agree with those who maintain that the high-protection tariff policies of the United States are the sole or even the principal cause of the stagnation of world trade . . . But there is little doubt in my mind that no matter what those other causes are . . . the world-wide prevalence of high tariffs, quotas, embargoes, and similar trade restrictions stands in the way of a substantial resumption of world trade.

In Capper's view, if the United States wanted to expand world trade, it had few options other than to seek trade agreements with other countries:

[I]f we continue our present high-tariff rates, the other nations of the world will keep their high-tariff rates, and perhaps erect even some additional barriers against us. It seems to me equally evident that if the United States reduces its tariff walls on its own, our markets will be swamped with a devastating flood of foreign goods, without any compensating foreign markets for any of our own products on equitable tariff terms. It seems fairly obvious, then, that if world trade is to be stimulated and our own export trade is to be revived by means of changes in tariff schedules, reciprocal action by ourselves and other countries involved is absolutely necessary.

In this case, however, Capper did not see a direct role for Congress:

But if reciprocal trade agreements are to be negotiated, it does not look as if Congress, from the practical viewpoint, is qualified, or even able, to undertake the task.... our experience in writing tariff legislation, particularly in the postwar era, has been discouraging. Trading between groups and sections is inevitable. Logrolling is inevitable, and in its most pernicious form. We do not write a national tariff law. We jam together, through various unholy alliances and combinations, a potpourri or hodgepodge of section and local tariff rates, which often add to our troubles and increase world misery. For myself, I see no reason to believe that another attempt would result in a more happy ending. (*Congressional Record*, June 4, 1934, 10378–79)

One striking difference between the Smoot-Hawley tariff and the Reciprocal Trade Agreements Act was the utter lack of participation by interest groups trying to influence Congress when it considered the RTAA. In contrast to the voluminous hearings and other materials generated when Congress considered Smoot-Hawley, the Ways and Means Committee received only sixty-three pieces of RTAA-related correspondence, fifty-nine of which opposed the bill. Although cotton and wheat farmers supported the bill, textile firms, toy makers, and many others small and medium-sized producers opposed it (Schnietz 2000, 428). One reason for the lack of interest in the RTAA compared to Smoot-Hawley was that "in contrast to 1930 . . . when interest groups were the

STILL HOVERING AROUND THE SENATE

Source: *St. Louis Post-Dispatch* Editorial Cartoon Collection. Courtesy of the State Historical Society of Missouri.

main protagonists and specific tariff rates the issue, the most important issues at stake in 1934 were institutional, centering on the transfer of authority from Congress to the executive" (Haggard 1988, 112). The RTAA was legislation that enabled presidential authority. No one knew how the authority would be used, how successful the negotiations would be, how extensive any agreements might be, which interests might be most affected, or whether it would be sustained by future Congresses. It was not obvious that the RTAA would necessarily produce a lasting, durable change in trade policy, but it did indicate that the Democratic Congress was willing to forego the business of tariff logrolling and take a more limited role in the making of trade policy.

Like Smoot-Hawley, the RTAA did not originate primarily because of the demands of interest groups. Of course, some key economic interests supported the legislation, but they did not directly instigate it. Rather, when the Democrats replaced the Republicans, the interests represented in Washington changed: instead of the import-competing producers championed by Republicans, the Democrats tried to help export-oriented farmers and manufacturers. The politicians took the lead in expanding the foreign market for America's agricultural and manufactured goods, but did not act in direct response to lobbying by those interests. Democratic politicians and administration officials pushed the idea of reciprocal trade agreements, and then sought to garner the support of important constituencies behind the idea. Like Smoot-Hawley itself, this suggests that politicians can use economic interests to achieve their political goals, and that a country's tariff policy is not just the result of economic interests manipulating pliable politicians for their own benefit.

Throughout the 1930s, Cordell Hull's State Department reached trade agreements with more than a dozen countries and this began to whittle down U.S. tariffs. The Democratic Congress renewed the RTAA in 1937 and 1940 over the fierce objections of Republicans. The trade agreements program culminated in the negotiation of the multilateral General Agreement on Tariffs and Trade (GATT) in 1947. The GATT consisted of a set of rules governing trade policy and negotiated tariff reductions, and thereby established the postwar world trading system.[3] A leading principle of the GATT was non-discrimination in the form of the unconditional most-favored nation clause (MFN). American insistence on unconditional MFN is consistent with the idea that it had been motivated by an effort to roll back the discriminatory policies that arose in Smoot-Hawley's wake. In fact, U.S. negotiators were "far more interested in the elimination or reduction of the bound margins of preference in favor of British countries than in [the] reduction of the United Kingdom's most-favored-foreign-nation tariff," according to State Department documents at the time (Dur 2010, 80).

Indeed, although the GATT was founded seventeen years after the passage of the Smoot-Hawley tariff, that earlier act had not been forgotten. Harking back to the early 1930s, President Harry Truman (1963, 168) lay out some of the reasons for the importance of the agreement:

> As each battle of the economic war of the thirties was fought, the inevitable tragic result be-

---

[3] On the origins of the GATT, see Irwin, Mavroidis, and Sykes (2008).

came more and more apparent. From the tariff policy of Hawley and Smoot, the world went on to Ottawa and the system of imperial preferences, from Ottawa to the kind of elaborate and detailed restrictions adopted by Nazi Germany. Nations strangled normal trade and discriminated against their neighbors, all around the world. Who among their peoples were the gainers? Not the depositors who lost their savings in the failure of the banks. Not the farmers who lost their farms. Not the millions who walked the streets looking for work. I do not mean to say that economic conflict was the *sole* cause of the depression. But I do say that it was a *major* cause.

Republicans unanimously opposed the RTAA during the 1930s, but, after World War II, they were split in their opposition (Irwin and Kroszner 1999). Most Republicans shed their isolationist past and became wary internationalists. They worried about giving too much discretionary power to the president to reduce tariff rates, but after the laborious experience of drafting the Smoot-Hawley tariff, no one in Congress—not even Republicans—wanted to assume direct responsibility for setting tariff rates again. Sen. Arthur Vandenberg (R-MI), a former isolationist who had voted in favor of Smoot-Hawley and against the RTAA repeatedly during the 1930s, reminded his colleagues:

> Tariff-rate making in Congress is atrocious. It lacks any element of economic science or validity. I suspect the 10 members of the Senate,

including myself, who struggled through the 11 months it took to write the last congressional tariff act, would join me in resigning before they would be willing to tackle another general congressional tariff revision. (*Congressional Record*, June 14, 1948, 8049–50)

And Robert Taft, the influential Republican Senator from Ohio who opposed the reciprocal trade agreements approach even after the war, wrote: "I stated that I was not in favor of returning to the fixing of tariff rates by Congress which inevitably brought about a serious logrolling procedure, but I favored a tariff board authorized to fix tariffs according to some standard prescribed by Congress having some relation to difference in the cost of production in the United States and abroad" (Taft 2006, 3: 228–29).

Yet some Republicans remained nostalgic for high protective tariffs even into the early 1950s. Shortly after taking office in 1953, President Dwight Eisenhower met with Republican congressional leaders. Coming from the more liberal, internationalist wing of the Republican Party, Eisenhower discovered that he had many disagreements with the more conservative members of his party in Congress on issues such as trade. Eisenhower (1963, 195) recalled that some congressional Republicans "were unhappy with the Trade Agreements Act, and a few even hoped we could restore the Smoot-Hawley Tariff Act, a move which I knew would be ruinous."

By this time, however, only a small minority of Republicans seriously wanted a return to the tariff policies of Smoot and Hawley. Although there were partisan disagreements about the specific rules to be included in trade agreements, both parties endorsed the idea that the executive branch should be able to conclude trade agreements with other countries. As a result, the Tariff Act of 1930 proved to be the last time Congress ever determined the specific rates of duty that applied to U.S. imports.

INVOKING SMOOT AND HAWLEY

Since World War II, a series of multilateral and bilateral trade agreements have reduced U.S. tariffs to levels that would have shocked Smoot and Hawley. Whereas the average tariff on dutiable imports was 45 percent in 1930, it was less than 5 percent in 2010. Since World War II, presidents and other members of Congress have repeatedly invoked Smoot-Hawley and the experience of the 1930s to reject calls for protectionism and to justify the continued movement toward freer trade.

For example, in December 1967, upon signing the Kennedy Round trade agreements negotiated under the GATT, President Lyndon Johnson (1968, 2: 1150) said:

> What captain of industry or what union leader in this country really yearns and is eager to return to the days of Smoot-Hawley? For the world of higher tariffs, and quotas, and competitive currency depreciation was also the world of you-know-what—deep depressions, rampant unemployment, low profits, if any, and, generally, losses.

Johnson argued that any move to raise tariffs would "set a chain reaction of counter-protection and retaliation that would put in jeopardy our ability to work together and to prosper together" and that the days of "declining trade barriers in a world of unprecedented prosperity and growth is something we want to continue."

The politics of U.S. trade policy changed significantly over the postwar period. Imports had little impact on the economy during the 1950s and 1960s, so trade policy was not very contentious. But imports began to grow rapidly in the 1970s and 1980s as Europe and Japan fully recovered from World War II and other countries emerged as important producers. As foreign competition intensified, protectionist pressures reemerged and trade policy once again became a controversial issue.

In the early 1970s, Congress considered (but failed to pass) a bill that would have imposed quotas on imported textiles, apparel, and other goods. Opponents warned that protectionist measures would risk repeating the errors of the 1930s. Rep. Sam Gibbons (D-FL) reminded his colleagues that "I think all of us know, and as history has taught us, what a sorry mistake the Smoot-Hawley Act was." Gibbons said that Smoot-Hawley was "a horrible monstrosity" that "helped pull this country down into the very depths of the depression. . . . those of us who were old enough to remember realize that Smoot-Hawley was probably one of the main causes of the disintegration of world trade that took place then, and it led to World War II with the tremendous loss of life during that war" (*Congressional Record*, December 10, 1973, 40498–99).

Even more severe protectionist pressures emerged in the early 1980s. The United States was hit with a painful recession and high unemployment, along with intensified foreign competition in key industries such as automobiles and steel and a growing trade deficit as the dollar appreciated against other major currencies. Congress repeatedly considered, and sometimes passed, legislation to limit imports of textiles, steel, automobiles, and other goods. Those defending open trade policies frequently invoked Smoot-Hawley to argue against any protectionist action. Few did so as often as President Ronald Reagan, who vetoed the trade-restricting legislation. For example, in 1983, in one of his radio addresses, he said:

> There's a great hue and cry for us to bend to protectionist pressures. Well, I've been around long enough to remember that when we did that once before in this century, something called Smoot-Hawley, we lived through a nightmare. World trade fell by 60 percent, contributing to the Great Depression and to the political turmoil that led to World War II. (Reagan 1984, 1: 332)[4]

Reagan made similar statements at many points during his administration. In 1985, he said:

> [S]ome of us remember the 1930s, when the most destructive trade bill in history, the Smoot-Hawley tariff act, helped plunge this nation and the world into a decade of depression and despair. From now on, if the ghost of Smoot-Hawley rears its ugly head in Congress, if Congress crafts a depression-making bill, I'll fight it. (Reagan 1988, 2: 1032)

As they debated trade legislation throughout the 1980s, members of Congress had many occasions to remember

---

[4] The value of world trade did fall that much in nominal terms, partly due to deflation and partly due to the fall in the volume of trade.

Smoot and Hawley. By this time, however, the political parties had switched positions on trade: Republicans supported open international trade and the Democrats supported limiting imports to help domestic industries producing similar goods.[5] Republicans began invoking Smoot-Hawley as a way of warning about the outcome of protectionist trade policies. Sen. John Chafee (R-RI) claimed that Smoot-Hawley, "without question, led to the Great Depression" (*Congressional Record*, June 17, 1985, 15975). Even those Republicans who advocated an aggressive stance against unfair foreign trade practices conceded the point. One such advocate, Sen. John Danforth (R-MO), stated:

> The Smoot-Hawley tariff did contribute to the Great Depression. To repeat the same mistake more than half a century later would be an act of gross stupidity. The goal of the United States should be to open markets, not to close them. (*New York Times*, April 25, 1985, 9429)

Some Democrats continued to share this view. Sen. Daniel Patrick Moynihan (D-NY) stated that "there has never been as disastrous a piece of economic legislation" as Smoot-Hawley because it "helped bring on 10 years of miserable depression" (*Congressional Record*, July 30, 1982, 18575).

Other Democrats rejected the Smoot-Hawley analogy and strove to refute the charge that Smoot-Hawley had

[5] This is partly because the two parties have switched the region of the country from which they draw their political support. Unlike the 1920s, the Republicans now drew their support from the South and West, whereas the Democrats now drew their political strength from the North. See Keech and Pak (2005).

led to the Great Depression. The two senators who frequently sought to correct the "myth" of Smoot-Hawley were Sen. John Heinz (D-PA) and Sen. Ernest Hollings (D-SC).[6] They repeatedly argued that Smoot-Hawley was not responsible for the collapse in trade or the Great Depression. As Heinz said, "Smoot-Hawley seems to be a favorite example of these free traders; never mind that the effects of it could not possibly have been felt before the fall of 1930 and by then the Depression was well underway, that it covered less than 1 percent of world trade, that in 1930–32 duty free imports into the United Sates fell at almost the same percentage rate as dutiable imports" (*Congressional Record*, September 30, 1985, 25310). He claimed that the effects of Smoot-Hawley had been exaggerated and that it had been made "the scapegoat for the Great Crash, notwithstanding the fact that it was not enacted until nine months later, the entire Depression, World War II, and no doubt the decline of the nuclear family as the basic element of American society" (*Congressional Record*, December 3, 1987, 33969).

As part of his efforts to defend the Smoot-Hawley tariff, Heinz inserted a study—"The Myth of Smoot-Hawley" —into the *Congressional Record* three times. Heinz did so because "every time someone in the Congress gives a speech about a more aggressive trade policy or the need to confront our trading partners with their subsidies, barriers to imports and other unfair practices, others, often in the academic community or in the Congress, immediately react with speeches on the return of Smoot-Hawley and the dark days of blatant protectionism. . . . Smoot-

---

[6] Not surprisingly, they represented states that had been hit hard by foreign competition in the 1980s, steel in the case of Pennsylvania and textile and apparel in the case of South Carolina.

Hawley has thus become a code word for protectionism, and in turn a code word for depression and a major economic disaster." Heinz rejected this view and sought to remind members of Congress that

> historians and economists, who usually view these things objectively, realize that the truth is a good deal more complicated, that the causes of the depression were far deeper, and that the link between high tariffs and economic disaster is much more tenuous than is implied by this simplistic linkage. . . . This of course is not to suggest that high tariffs are good or that Smoot-Hawley was a wise piece of legislation. It was not. But it was also clearly not responsible for all the ills of the 1930s that are habitually blamed on it by those who fancy themselves defenders of free trade. (*Congressional Record*, May 9, 1983, 11538–39)

Sen. Ernest "Fritz" Hollings was even more colorful in his rejection of the standard invocation of Smoot-Hawley. With his deep baritone voice and rich Southern accent, the loquacious Hollings drew frequent comparisons to the rooster "Foghorn Leghorn" from Bugs Bunny cartoons. Hollings criticized existing trade policies and said:

> the advocates of so-called free trade have confected an elaborate and colorful mythology. They sing hallelujahs to the "invisible hand" and genuflect before the altar of "comparative advantage" . . . Of course, the "free traders" also have a demonology. And the Mephistopheles

and Lucifer of that hyper-imaginative demon-
ology are Representative Will Hawley and
Senator Reed Smoot, coauthors of the famous
tariff act that bears their names. For decades,
we have been regaled with the fable of the
dastardly Hawley-Smoot tariffs, and how they
precipitate the Great Crash of 1929. Well, Mr.
President, let the record show that the economic crash allegedly precipitated by Hawley-
Smoot happened in 1929. It is an inconvenient
fact that Hawley-Smoot was passed and took
effect in 1930. There are many other inconvenient facts about Hawley-Smoot, facts that fail
to conform to the popular mythology. (*Congressional Record*, July 14, 1987, 19765)

The way in which the Smoot-Hawley tariff was
used in the trade debate changed subtly over time. In
the 1980s, it was invoked to argue against the raising
of trade barriers. By the 1990s, it was invoked to argue
against those who opposed the reduction of trade barriers. The names of Smoot and Hawley came up several
times during the NAFTA debate in 1993, especially with
Vice President Al Gore's memorable episode during the
televised debate with Ross Perot. They received further
attention the following year in the debate over the Uruguay Round agreements that created the World Trade
Organization.[7] In a representative statement, Sen. John
Breaux (D-LA) said:

---

[7] In August 1994, a group of 446 economists sent a letter to President Bill
Clinton supporting the Uruguay Round agreement. Three of the economists
who signed the letter had also signed the 1930 letter to President Hoover that
warned against passage of the Smoot-Hawley tariff.

Today's vote is a vote between—and a choice between—old versus new. It is a question of whether we want to return to the days of the Smoot-Hawley tariff or whether we want to march into the 21st century. It is a question of whether we build walls around the United States or whether we tear down the walls around other countries of the world. (*Congressional Record*, December 1, 1994, 30159)

But those suspicious of the WTO and increased trade, such as Sen. James Exon (D-NE), countered:

The proponents of this agreement will try to portray the opponents as protectionist. The choice is not between the World Trade Organization and Smoot-Hawley. There are a number of other options. (*Congressional Record*, December 1, 1994, 30160)

Sen. Max Baucus (D-MT) added that "I hear all of these horror stories that if this is not approved, the world is going to come to an end, a cataclysmic response, Smoot-Hawley. . . . it is all baloney. It is untrue. (*Congressional Record*, November 29, 1994, 29971)

Smoot-Hawley received mention in smaller but still divisive trade debates over granting permanent normalized trade relations (PNTR) to China and granting trade preferences to Africa in 2000. Sen. Charles Grassley (R-IA) suggested that, if Congress did not agree to these measures, then

I suppose you could go back to the 1930s, when
we learned the lesson of the Smoot-Hawley
legislation that brought about the world depression, and the world depression brought
about World War II. We very quickly learned
that high tariffs are not good for the world
economy. It was not good for the American
economy because we suffered as much or more
than they did elsewhere in the world in that
Great Depression as a result of Smoot-Hawley.
(*Congressional Record*, May 10, 2000, S3789)

Such statements irritated Sen. Fritz Hollings, who recalled his efforts with Sen. Heinz in the 1980s to educate
Congress about how the impact of Smoot-Hawley had
been blown out of proportion:

We were tired of hearing about Smoot-Hawley,
and that the hobgoblins were coming.... Then
the talk was that Smoot-Hawley would cause
a world war; if you do not vote for this we are
going to have World War III. I never heard of
such nonsense. It is time we jailed that buzzard,
Smoot-Hawley. (*Congressional Record*, September 7, 2000, S8153)

Hollings argued that Americans needed to "start talking [about trade] as realists. And quit giving us these symbolic baloneys, malarkeys such as Smoot-Hawley" (*Congressional Record*, September 10, 1996, 22513).

More than eighty years after the tariff was imposed,
Smoot and Hawley are still mentioned in Congress and

Name the most

✴ DEPRESSING COUPLE ✴
in U.S. history.

Rep. Hawley & Sen. Smoot

Our vote goes to Hawley and Smoot, the misguided legislators whose protectionist trade tariffs prolonged the Great Depression. Retaliation by our trade partners caused U.S. exports to plummet. Imports fell by more than two-thirds. The GDP fell by 50%. Unemployment rose from 9% to 25%. Amazing that two misguided individuals and one bad idea could spark the most depressing economic

—Fig A.—
Dow Jones Industrial Average, 1929

chain reaction of the 20th century.

✴ ✴ ✴ ✴

It was misguided policy in 1930, and it's misguided policy now. Keep Americans working, and keep our economy the strongest in the world. Don't repeat history. Support free trade agreements with Colombia, Panama and Korea. Reauthorize Trade Promotion Authority.

This 2008 newspaper ad by the Consumer Electronics Association reminded readers of the Smoot-Hawley tariff in seeking support for free trade agreements with Panama, Colombia, and South Korea. Source: CEA. www.ce.org

in newspaper editorials when the debate turns to trade.[8]
But as time passes, the story sometimes gets distorted.
In 2009, Rep. Michele Bachmann (R-MN) made one of
the more amusing invocations of Smoot-Hawley when
she stated that "the Hoot-Smalley act, which was a tremendous burden on tariff restrictions, and then of course
trade barriers and the regulatory burden and tax barriers.
That's what we saw happen under FDR that took a recession and blew it into a full scale depression."[9] Of course,
Smoot-Hawley occurred under President Hoover, not
President Roosevelt.

Could Smoot-Hawley Return Again?

The reminders of the dark days of the early 1930s have
been a check on Congress reasserting itself into the realm
of trade policy. Smoot and Hawley have been the bogey

[8] Sen. John McCain (R-AZ):

In 1930, as the United States and the world were entering what would
be known in history as the Great Depression, two men, Mr. Smoot and
Mr. Hawley, led the effort to enact protectionist legislation in the face
of economic crisis. Their bill, the Smoot-Hawley Tariff Act, raised duties on thousands of imported goods in a futile attempt to keep jobs at
home. In the face of this legislation, 1,028 economists issued a statement
to President Herbert Hoover, wherein they wrote: "America is now facing the problem of unemployment. . . . The proponents of higher tariffs
would claim that an increase in rates will give work to the idle. This is not
true. We cannot increase employment by restricting trade." Mr. Smoot,
Mr. Hawley, and their colleagues paid no attention to this wise admon-
ishment, and the Congress went ahead with protectionist legislation. In
doing so, they sparked an international trade war as countries around the
world retaliated, raising their own duties and restricting trade, and they
helped turn a severe recession into the greatest depression in modern history. (*Congressional Record*, March 18, 2009, S3331)

[9] Speech on House floor, April 27, 2009, transcribed from cspan.org. In the
Congressional Record, the names of Smoot and Hawley were corrected, April 27,
2009, H4762.

men of protectionist trade policy and serve as a warning
of what can happen when protectionism gets out of control. As Harvard economist Richard Cooper (1987, 292)
has argued:

> Valuable lessons were learned from the Smoot-
> Hawley tariff experience by the foreign policy
> community: the threat of tariff retaliation is
> not always merely a bluff; tariffs do influence
> trade flows negatively; a decline in trade can
> depress national economies; economic de-
> pression provides fertile ground for politically
> radical nostrums; and political radicals often
> seek foreign (military) adventures to distract
> domestic attention away from their domestic
> economic failures. The seeds of World War
> II, in both the Far East and in Europe, were
> sowed by Hoover's signing of the Smoot-
> Hawley tariff.

While this description may be a stretch, it is more accurate than the claim that Smoot-Hawley had no impact
on trade and did not contribute to the problems of the
period.

But what happens as historical memories fade and
Smoot-Hawley no longer has the power to instill the fear
of protectionism and trade wars? Could the United States
ever return to the protectionist days of Smoot-Hawley?
The U.S. financial crisis in 2008 and subsequent sharp
recession had some early, and eerie, parallels to the onset
of the Great Depression. This prompted fears that there
might be a similar outbreak of protectionism (Evenett,
Hoekman, and Cattaneo 2009). Fortunately, such an out-

come is unlikely. The American political system has enormous inertia and a high degree of status-quo bias. It took a Great Depression and World War II to dislodge a high-tariff regime from its secure position in the American political system. It would take another enormous shock for the United States to turn its back on the system of open trade that it helped to create after World War II and has cultivated ever since.

There are several specific reasons to discount the likelihood of returning to the days of Smoot-Hawley. First, Congress tried to use protective tariffs to help agriculture and industry in the 1920s because, at that time, the range of available policy instruments was limited. There were no subsidies or social safety nets to help American farmers, so politicians resorted to the only policy available–higher import duties. Today, there are many forms of income support, including trade adjustment assistance and unemployment insurance, that help workers adversely affected by imports or an economic downturn.

Furthermore, during the Depression, the fixed exchange rates of the gold standard prevented the use of monetary policy to help the economy. Operating on the belief that budgets should be balanced even during recessions, most governments in the 1930s did not use fiscal policy as a potential stabilization tool either. With monetary and fiscal policy responses ruled out, governments resorted to the only policy instrument at their disposal—import restrictions—to give the economy a boost. Understanding those constraints on policy instruments goes a long way to explaining why the 1930s was such a disastrous period for trade policies around the world (Eichengreen and Irwin 2010). Today, of course, governments have a wide variety of policy tools to address economic downturns and trade interventions have been largely, but not wholly, taken off the table.

Second, the United States is much more engaged in world trade today than it was in the 1920s and 1930s. In 1929, exports of goods and services were only about 5 percent of GDP. Today, exports are 11 percent of GDP. This has occurred despite the fact that the economy has shifted toward services, and agriculture and manufacturing are much less important now than they were then. The fact that trade is a larger percentage of GDP means that an outbreak of protectionism is potentially more disruptive to the U.S. economy than in the past. The United States has a greater stake in open markets at home and abroad because its economy is much more economically integrated with the world than in the past.

Third, the exchange rate regime matters for the ability to use trade policies to affect macroeconomic outcomes. Under fixed exchange rates, if a devaluation is ruled out, there is a potential macroeconomic benefit from protection. As chapter 2 noted, a higher tariff with a fixed exchange rate could lead to an increase in net exports or an increase in central bank reserves, either of which might provide some short-term stimulus to the economy, assuming no foreign retaliation. After the breakdown of the Bretton Woods system in the early 1970s, the world shifted from a fixed exchange rate regime to a floating exchange rate regime. Flexible exchange rates allow a country to have a strong monetary policy response to an economic downturn without resorting to protection. In addition, a tariff is generally ineffective under floating exchange rates: it reduces spending on imports, but also leads to an appreciation of the domestic currency, which diminishes exports and negates any stimulative effect on domestic output. As Paul Krugman (1982, 178) has noted: "the general presumption . . . is that tariffs and quotas are likely to have a contractionary effect under a regime of floating exchange rates."[10] Hence, the potential macroeconomic benefits of protectionism under fixed exchange rates do not exist under floating exchange rates.

Finally, U.S. trade policy prior to 1934 was completely unilateral and did not take into account the reaction of foreign trade partners. Congress was only dimly concerned about the threat of retaliation and did not take such considerations very seriously. Today, the United States knows with certainty that any breach of international trade rules on its part will lead to retaliation against its exports. In fact, this retaliation is now built into the world trading system of the WTO. Under the WTO's dispute settlement system, countries are permitted to retaliate against those found to have violated international trade agreements. Once again, any perceived advantage from limiting imports will have to be balanced against the very real cost of lost exports. This threat has been used to punish those deviating from international agreements and has successfully served as a check on opportunistic behavior (Bown 2004a, 2004b).[11]

[10] As Krugman continues: "The effects of a tariff on money demand and the effects of real appreciation on spending suggest that the indirect effects of protection will have a depressing effect on aggregate demand which more than offsets the direct effect of a tariff in switching expenditure onto domestic goods. . . . If nationalistic protection gives rise to a trade war, the conventional microeconomic losses from restricted trade will probably be dwarfed by severe macroeconomic losses as output contracts around the world."

[11] In 1995, the GATT became the World Trade Organization (WTO). A picture of Smoot and Hawley hangs in the office of Pascal Lamy, the director-general of the WTO in Geneva. Few people recognize them and Lamy is often asked if they are family relatives. See Lamy's speech, Reconciling America with an

For all of these reasons, it seems unlikely that the United States will return to the trade policies of Smoot and Hawley.

SUMMING UP

To conclude, the Smoot-Hawley tariff is an iconic piece of congressional legislation that still resonates in contemporary debates over trade policy. Its effects have been exaggerated by those who warn against the dangers of protectionism and minimized by those who wish to downplay the costs of deviating from free-trade policies. What have we learned from revisiting the history of the period?

The Smoot-Hawley tariff was an unnecessary piece of legislation, indeed a futile one. It could not achieve its ostensible objective of raising agricultural prices and helping farmers. The United States was a large net exporter of key crops (cotton, wheat and other grains, and tobacco) and those farmers could not be helped by a tariff on imports. Many agricultural imports did not compete with domestic production, and those that did (aside from sugar and wool, which were already heavily taxed) affected a relatively small number of farmers. Hence, the tariff could not achieve its goal. In addition, the political process surrounding the tariff revision gave congressional trade politics a deservedly bad name. As members of Congress noted, the tariff bill was a mass of private legislation carried out with little regard for national interest.

open trading system, Washington, DC, 24 April 2009, available at: http://www.wto.org/english/news_e/sppl_e/sppl122_e.htm. Accessed June 16, 2010.

The question of the economic consequences of the Smoot-Hawley tariff remains controversial. The tariff clearly reduced U.S. imports. Although the decline in demand due to the fall in income was the primary reason for the contraction in U.S. imports between 1929 and 1933, higher tariffs were also a significant factor. The Smoot-Hawley tariff did not cause the Great Depression. It did not ameliorate it through a monetary channel (an inflow of monetary gold) or a Keynesian channel (switching expenditures from foreign to domestic goods). In part because Smoot-Hawley led to retaliation and discrimination against the United States, exports fell more than imports. Real net exports were a drag on the economy during the Depression itself and during the first years of the recovery. Thus, it can be said that Smoot-Hawley made the Depression worse for the United States than it might otherwise have been.

The question of the international consequences of the Smoot-Hawley tariff is also controversial. Although the tariff was not the principal reason for the general outbreak of protectionism that so damaged world trade in the early 1930s, it was a contributing factor. However, several countries retaliated directly or indirectly against the United States, especially Canada, the country's largest trading partner. Canada's response by itself had a large and adverse effect on U.S. exports. But the real damage came from the fact that the resentment caused by Smoot-Hawley led other countries to form preferential trading blocs that discriminated against the United States. Discrimination against U.S. goods in export markets, notably imperial preferences, diverted world trade away from the

IT BACKFIRED BEFORE

Source: *St. Louis Post-Dispatch* Editorial Cartoon Collection. Courtesy of the State Historical Society of Missouri.

United States and made the economic recovery from the Great Depression more difficult.

In the end, we can conclude that the stigma of Smoot-Hawley is well deserved. It failed to achieve its domestic goal of helping farmers and it backfired against the United States around the world. It should always be remembered as a warning about the adverse consequences of poorly considered trade policies.

Appendix

The Economists' Statement against the Smoot-Hawley Tariff

THE FOLLOWING STATEMENT was organized by Clair Wilcox of Swarthmore College and Paul H. Douglas of the University of Chicago and later a senator from Illinois. Fetter (1942) describes the origins of the statement, which cost a total of $140 to circulate to members of the American Economic Association. Most of the signatories were academic economists from 179 colleges and universities, including 28 signers from Columbia University, 26 from the University of Chicago, 25 from Harvard University, and 24 from Dartmouth College. Douglas (1972, 71) later wrote: "I think poor Hoover wanted to take our advice. His party was so strongly committed to protection, however, that he felt compelled to sign the bill, with the result that all our predictions came true." Sen. Daniel Patrick Moynihan said of the list: "It is a role of honor to this profession of economics" (*Congressional Record*, July 30, 1982, 18758). The text is taken from the *Congressional Record*, May 5, 1930, pages 8327–28.

• • •

The undersigned American economists and teachers of economics strongly urge that any measure which provides for a general upward revision of tariff rates be denied passage by Congress, or if passed, be vetoed by the President.

We are convinced that increased protective duties would be a mistake. They would operate, in general, to increase the prices which domestic consumers would have to pay. By raising prices they would encourage concerns with higher costs to undertake production, thus compelling the consumer to subsidize waste and inefficiency in industry. At the same time they would force him to pay higher rates of profit to established firms which enjoyed lower production costs. A higher level of protection, such as is contemplated by both the House and Senate bills, would therefore raise the cost of living and injure the great majority of our citizens.

Few people could hope to gain from such a change. Miners, construction, transportation and public utility workers, professional people and those employed in banks, hotels, newspaper offices, in the wholesale and retail trades, and scores of other occupations would clearly lose, since they produce no products which could be protected by tariff barriers.

The vast majority of farmers, also, would lose. Their cotton, corn, lard, and wheat are export crops and are sold in the world market. They have no important competition in the home market. They can not benefit, therefore, from any tariff which is imposed upon the basic commodities which they produce. They would lose through the increased duties on manufactured goods, however, and in a double fashion. First, as consumers they would have to pay still higher prices for the products, made of textiles, chemicals, iron, and steel, which they buy. Second, as producers, their ability to sell their products would be further restricted by the barriers placed in the way of foreigners who wished to sell manufactured goods to us.

Our export trade, in general, would suffer. Countries can not permanently buy from us unless they are permitted to sell to us, and the more we restrict the importation of goods from them by means of ever higher tariffs the more we reduce the possibility of our exporting to them. This applies to such exporting industries as copper, automobiles, agricultural machinery, typewriters, and the like fully as much as it does to farming. The difficulties of these industries are likely to be increased still further if we pass a higher tariff. There are already many evidences that such action would inevitably provoke other countries to pay us back in kind by levying retaliatory duties against our goods. There are few more ironical spectacles than that of the American Government as it seeks, on the one hand, to promote exports through the activity of the Bureau of Foreign and Domestic Commerce, while, on the other hand, by increasing tariffs it makes exportation ever more difficult. President Hoover has well said, in his message to Congress on April 16, 1929, "It is obviously unwise protection which sacrifices a greater amount of employment in exports to gain a less amount of employment from imports."

We do not believe that American manufacturers, in general, need higher tariffs. The report of the President's committee on recent economics changes has shown that industrial efficiency has increased, that costs have fallen, that profits have grown with amazing rapidity since the end of the war. Already our factories supply our people with over 96 percent of the manufactured goods which they consume, and our producers look to foreign markets to absorb the increasing output of their machines. Further barriers to trade will serve them not well, but ill.

Many of our citizens have invested their money in foreign enterprises. The Department of Commerce has estimated that such investments, entirely aside from the war debts, amounted to between $12,555,000,000 and $14,555,000,000 on January 1, 1929. These investors, too, would suffer if protective duties were to be increased, since such action would make it still more difficult for their foreign creditors to pay them the interest due them.

America is now facing the problem of unemployment. Her labor can find work only if her factories can sell their products. Higher tariffs would not promote such sales. We can not increase employment by restricting trade. American industry, in the present crisis, might well be spared the burden of adjusting itself to new schedules of protective duties.

Finally, we would urge our Government to consider the bitterness which a policy of higher tariffs would inevitably inject into our international relations. The United States was ably represented at the World Economic Conference which was held under the auspices of the League of Nations in 1927. This conference adopted a resolution announcing that "the time has come to put an end to the increase in tariffs and move in the opposite direction." The higher duties proposed in our pending legislation violate the spirit of this agreement and plainly invite other nations to compete with us in raising further barriers to trade. A tariff war does not furnish good soil for the growth of world peace.

ORIGINATORS AND FIRST SIGNERS

PAUL H. DOUGLAS, professor of economics,
University of Chicago.

IRVING FISHER, professor of economics,
Yale University.

FRANK D. GRAHAM, professor of economics,
Princeton University.

ERNEST M. PATTERSON, professor of economics,
University of Pennsylvania.

HENRY R. SEAGER, professor of economics,
Columbia University.

FRANK W. TAUSSIG, professor of economics,
Harvard University.

CLAIR WILCOX, associate professor of economics,
Swarthmore College.

*[There followed the signatures and affiliations of more than a
thousand economists from around the country.]*

Acknowledgments

THERE ARE MANY PEOPLE who deserve thanks for their help with this book. Michael Bordo, Barry Eichengreen, Anne Krueger, Elias Papaioannou, and Peter Temin provided helpful comments on various sections. The external reviewers—Harold James, Kris Mitchener, and Robert Whaples—provided very useful feedback on an early draft. John Conklin, the government documents librarian at Dartmouth College, provided invaluable support in gaining access to many official publications. Todd Minsk and everyone at the Baker/Berry Library Circulation Desk kept a shelf open for me, ready to handle my frequent requests from the storage library. Diana Wyman of Statistics Canada graciously contributed some data used in chapter 3. Rebecca Kohn provided expert editorial assistance with the manuscript and improved it considerably. Seth Ditchik and his great team at Princeton University Press, including Leslie Grundfest, Janie Chan, and Karen Verde, helped shepherd the book through the review and publication process.

This book is dedicated to my father for having introduced me to the magical kingdom of the library, a place where it is impossible to become bored.

References

Alston, Lee. 1983. "Farm Foreclosures in the United States During the Interwar Period." *Journal of Economic History* 43, 445–57.

Archibald, Robert B., and David H. Feldman. 1998. "Investment during the Great Depression: Uncertainty and the Role of Smoot-Hawley Tariff." *Southern Economic Journal* 64, 857–79.

Archibald, Robert B., David H. Feldman, Marc D. Hayford, and Carl A. Pasurka. 2000. "Effective Rates of Protection and the Fordney-McCumber and Smoot-Hawley Tariff Acts: Comment and Revised Estimates." *Applied Economics* 32, 1223–26.

Bailey, Michael, Judith Goldstein, and Barry Weingast. 1997. "The Institutional Roots of American Trade Policy: The Origin and Effects of the Reciprocal Trade Agreements Act." *World Politics* 49, 309–38.

Barry, Dave. 1990. *Dave Barry Slept Here: A Sort of History of the United States*. New York: Random House.

Bernanke, Ben. 1983. "Non-Monetary Effects of the Financial Crisis in the Propagation of the Great Depression." *American Economic Review* 73, 257–76.

———. 1995. "The Macroeconomics of the Great Depression: A Comparative Approach." *Journal of Money, Credit and Banking* 27, 1–28.

Bidwell, Percy W. 1930. "The New American Tariff: Europe's Answer." *Foreign Affairs* 9, 13–26.

Bierman, Harold, Jr. 1998. *The Causes of the 1929 Stock Market Crash*. Westport, CT: Greenwood Press.

Bordo, Michael, Ehsan Choudhri, and Anna Schwartz. 2002. "Was Expansionary Monetary Policy Feasible during the Great Contraction? An Examination of the Gold Standard Constraint." *Explorations in Economic History* 39, 1–28.

Bown, Chad P. 2004a. "Trade Disputes and the Implementation of Protection under the GATT: An Empirical Assessment." *Journal of International Economics* 62, 263–94.

———. 2004b. "On the Economic Success of GATT/WTO Dispute Settlement." *Review of Economics and Statistics* 86, 811–23.

Boyce, Robert. 2009. *The Great Interwar Crisis and the Collapse of Globalization*. New York: Palgrave Macmillan.

Buchanan, Patrick J. 1998. *The Great Betrayal: How American Sovereignty and Social Justice Are Being Sacrificed to the Gods of the Global Economy*. Boston: Little & Brown.

Burner, David. 1979. *Herbert Hoover: A Public Life*. New York: Knopf.

Callahan, Colleen, Judith McDonald, and Anthony O'Brien. 1994. "Who Voted for Smoot-Hawley?" *Journal of Economic History* 54, 683–90.

Carey, Kevin. 1999. "Investigating a Debt Channel for the Smoot-Hawley Tariffs: Evidence from the Sovereign Bond Market." *Journal of Economic History* 59, 748–61.

Carter, Susan B., and Richard Sutch, eds. 2006. *Historical Statistics of the United States: Millennial Edition*. New York: Cambridge University Press.

Cole, Harold L., and Lee E. Ohanian. 1999. "The Great Depression in the United States from a Neoclassical Perspective." *Federal Reserve Bank of Minneapolis Quarterly Review* 23, 2–24.

———. 2007. "A Second Look at the U.S. Great Depression from a Neoclassical Perspective." In *Great Depressions of the Twentieth Century*, edited by Edward Prescott and Timothy Kehoe. Minneapolis: Federal Reserve Bank of Minneapolis.

Conner, James R. 1958. "National Farm Organizations and United States Tariff Policy in the 1920's." *Agricultural History* 32, 32–43.

Cooper, Richard N. 1987. "Trade Policy as Foreign Policy." In *U.S. Trade Relations in a Changing World Economy*, edited by Robert M. Stern. Cambridge: MIT Press.

Crucini, Mario J. 1994. "Sources of Variation in Real Tariff Rates: The United States, 1900–1940." *American Economic Review* 84, 732–43.

Crucini, Mario J., and James Kahn. 1996. "Tariffs and Aggregate Economic Activity: Lessons from the Great Depression." *Journal of Monetary Economics* 38, 427–67.

———. 2007. "Tariffs and the Great Depression Revisited." In *Great Depressions of the Twentieth Century*, edited by Edward Prescott and Timothy Kehoe. Minneapolis: Federal Reserve Bank of Minneapolis.

Cupitt, Richard, and Euel Elliott. 1994. "Schattschneider Revisited: Senate Voting on the Smoot-Hawley Tariff Act of 1930." *Economics and Politics* 6, 187–99.

Dornbusch, Rudiger, and Stanley Fischer. 1986. "The Open Economy: Implications for Monetary and Fiscal Policy." In *The American Business Cycle: Continuity and Change*, edited by Robert J. Gordon. Chicago: University of Chicago Press for the NBER.

Douglas, Paul H. 1972. *In the Fullness of Time*. New York: Harcourt Brace Jovanovich.

Dur, Andreas. 2010. *Protection for Exporters: Power and Discrimination in Transatlantic Trade Relations, 1930–2010*. Ithaca: Cornell University Press.

Dye, Alan, and Richard Sicotte. 2003. "The U.S. Sugar Tariff and the Cuban Revolution of 1933." Working Paper, Barnard College.

———. 2004. "The U.S. Sugar Program and the Cuban Revolution." *Journal of Economic History* 64, 673–704.

Eckes, Alfred E., Jr. 1995. *Opening America's Market: U.S. Foreign Trade Policy since 1776*. Chapel Hill: University of North Carolina Press.

———. 1998. "Smoot-Hawley and the Stock Market Crash, 1929–1930." *International Trade Journal* 12, 65–82.

Eggertsson, Gauti. 2008. "Great Expectations and the End of the Depression." *American Economic Review* 90, 1476–1516.

Eichengreen, Barry. 1989. "The Political Economy of the Smoot-Hawley Tariff." In *Research in Economic History*, edited by Roger Ransom. Vol. 12. Greenwich, CT: JAI Press.

———. 1992. *Golden Fetters: The Gold Standard and the Great Depression, 1919–1939*. New York: Oxford University Press.

Eichengreen, Barry, and Douglas A. Irwin. 2010. "The Slide to Protectionism in the Great Depression: Who Succumbed and Why?" *Journal of Economic History* 70, 872–98.

Eisenhower, Dwight D. 1963. *The White House Years: Mandate for Change, 1953–1956.* Garden City, NJ: Doubleday.

Evenett, Simon J., Bernard M. Hoekman, and Olivier Cattaneo. 2009. *Effective Crisis Response and Openness: Implications for the Trading System.* Washington, DC: World Bank.

Federico, Giovanni. 2005. "Not Guilty? Agriculture in the 1920s and the Great Depression." *Journal of Economic History* 65, 949–75.

Fetter, Frank W. 1933. "Congressional Tariff Theory." *American Economic Review* 23, 413–27.

———. 1942. "The Economists' Tariff Protest of 1930." *American Economic Review* 32, 355–56.

Feyrer, James. 2009. "Trade and Income: Exploiting Time Series Geography." NBER Working Paper No. 14910.

Fremling, Gertrud M. 1985. "Did the United States Transmit the Great Depression to the Rest of the World?" *American Economic Review* 75, 1181–85.

Friedman, Milton, and Anna J. Schwartz. 1963. *A Monetary History of the United States.* Princeton: Princeton University Press.

Glassford, Larry A. 1992. *Reaction and Reform: The Politics of the Conservative Party under R. B. Bennett, 1927–1938.* Toronto: University of Toronto Press.

Glickman, David L. 1947. "The British Imperial Preference System." *Quarterly Journal of Economics* 61, 439–70.

Gordon, Robert J. 1986. *The American Business Cycle.* Chicago: University of Chicago Press.

Haberler, Gottfried. 1976. *The World Economy, Money, and the Great Depression.* Washington, DC: American Enterprise Institute.

Haggard, Stephan. 1988. "The Institutional Foundations of Hegemony: Explaining the Reciprocal Trade Agreements Act of 1934." *International Organization* 42, 91–119.

Hall, Ray Ovid. 1933. "Smoot-Hawley Tariff Caused Only About $165,000,000 of 1931 Import Shrinkage." *The Annalist* (September 29): 403–4.

Hamilton, David E. 1985. "The Causes of the Banking Panic of 1930: Another View." *Journal of Southern History* 51, 581–608.

Hart, Michael. 2002. *A Trading Nation: Canadian Trade Policy from Colonialism to Globalization.* Vancouver: University of British Columbia Press.

Hawley, Willis C. 1930. "The New Tariff: A Defense." *Review of Reviews*, July.

Hayford, Marc, and Carl A. Pasurka, Jr. 1992. "The Political Economy of the Fordney-McCumber and Smoot-Hawley Tariff Acts." *Explorations in Economic History* 29, 30–50.

Hoover, Herbert. 1952. *Memoirs*. Vol. 2: The Cabinet and the Presidency, 1920–33. New York: Macmillan.

————. 1974. *Public Papers of the President of the United States*, 1929. Washington, DC: U.S. Government Printing Office.

————. 1976. *Public Papers of the President of the United States*, 1930. Washington, DC: U.S. Government Printing Office.

Hsieh, Chang-Tai, and Christina D. Romer. 2006. "Was the Federal Reserve Constrained by the Gold Standard during the Great Depression? Evidence from the 1932 Open Market Purchase Program." *Journal of Economic History* 66, 140–76.

Hull, Cordell. 1948. *Memoirs*. 2 vols. New York: Macmillan.

Irwin, Douglas A. 1998a. "Changes in U.S. Tariffs: The Role of Import Prices and Commercial Policies." *American Economic Review* 88, 1015–26.

————. 1998b. "The Smoot-Hawley Tariff: A Quantitative Assessment." *Review of Economics and Statistics* 80, 326–34.

————. 2010. "Trade Restrictiveness and Deadweight Losses from U.S. Tariffs." *American Economic Journal: Economic Policy* 2, 111–33.

Irwin, Douglas A., and Randall S. Kroszner. 1996. "Log-Rolling and Economic Interests in the Passage of the Smoot-Hawley Tariff." *Carnegie-Rochester Series on Public Policy* 45, 173–200.

————. 1999. "Interests, Institutions, and Ideology in Securing Policy Change: The Republican Conversion to Trade Liberalization after Smoot-Hawley." *Journal of Law and Economics* 42, 643–73.

Irwin, Douglas A., Petros C. Mavroidis, and Alan O. Sykes. 2008. *The Genesis of the GATT*. New York: Cambridge University Press.

Johnson, Lyndon B. 1968. *Public Papers of the President of the United States*, 1967. Washington, DC: Government Printing Office.

Jones, Joseph M. 1934. *Tariff Retaliation: Repercussions of the Hawley-Smoot Bill*. Philadelphia: University of Pennsylvania Press.

Keech, William R., and Kyoungsan Pak. 1995. "Partisanship, Institutions, and Change in American Trade Politics." *Journal of Politics* 57, 1130–42.

Kelley, Darwin N. 1940. "The McNary-Haugen Bills, 1924–1928: An Attempt to Make the Tariff Effective for Farm Products." *Agricultural History* 14, 170–80.

Kelley, William B., Jr. 1963. "Antecedents of Present Commercial Policy, 1922–1934." In *Studies in United States Commercial Policy*, edited by William B. Kelley, Jr. Chapel Hill: University of North Carolina Press.

Kindleberger, Charles P. 1986. *The World in Depression*. Revised edition. Berkeley: University of California Press.

Klingaman, William K. 1989. *1929: The Year of the Great Crash*. New York: Harper & Row.

Kottman, Richard N. 1968. *Reciprocity and the North American Triangle, 1932–1938*. Ithaca: Cornell University Press.

———. 1975. "Herbert Hoover and the Smoot-Hawley Tariff: Canada, a Case Study." *Journal of American History* 62, 609–35.

Koyama, Kumiko. 2009. "The Passage of the Smoot-Hawley Tariff Act: Why Did the President Sign the Bill?" *Journal of Policy History* 21, 163–86.

Krugman, Paul. 1982. "The Macroeconomics of Protection with a Floating Exchange Rate." *Carnegie-Rochester Series on Public Policy* 16, 141–82.

———. 1990. *The Age of Diminished Expectations: U.S. Economic Policy in the 1990s*. Cambridge: MIT Press.

Lamont, Thomas W. 1931. "Phases of the World Depression." *Proceedings of the Academy of Political Science* 14, 89–95.

Lary, Hal. 1943. *The United States in the World Economy*. Washington, DC: Government Printing Office.

League of Nations. 1931. "Evolution of Economic and Commercial Policy (Autonomous, Contractual and Collective) since the Tenth Assembly (June 19)." Geneva: League of Nations.

———. 1933. *World Economic Survey*. Geneva: League of Nations.

———. 1943. *Network of World Trade*. Geneva: League of Nations.

Leiter, Robert. 1961. "Organized Labor and the Tariff." *Southern Economic Journal* 28, 55–65.

Leuchtenburg, William E. 2009. *Herbert Hoover*. New York: Times Books.

Lucas, Robert E., Jr. 1994. "Review of Milton Friedman and Anna J. Schwartz's 'A Monetary History of the United States, 1867–1960.'" *Journal of Monetary Economics* 34, 5–16.

MacDougall, Donald, and Rosemary Hutt. 1954. "Imperial Preference: A Quantitative Analysis." *Economic Journal* 64, 233–57.

Madsen, Jakob B. 2001a. "Agricultural Crises and the International Transmission of the Great Depression." *Journal of Economic History* 61, 327–65.

———. 2001b. "Trade Barriers and the Collapse of World Trade during the Great Depression." *Southern Economic Journal* 67, 848–68.

Malin, James C. 1930. *The United States after the World War*. Boston: Ginn & Co.

Mankiw, N. Gregory. 2009. "It's No Time for Protectionism." *New York Times*, February 9.

McDonald, Judith A., Anthony Patrick O'Brien, and Colleen M. Callahan. 1997. "Tariff Wars: Canada's Reaction to the Smoot-Hawley Tariff." *Journal of Economic History* 57, 802–26.

Meltzer, Allan. H. 1976. "Monetary and Other Explanations of the Start of the Great Depression." *Journal of Monetary Economics* 2, 455–71.

———. 2003. *A History of the Federal Reserve. Vol.* 1: 1913–1951. Chicago: University of Chicago Press.

Merrill, Milton R. 1990. *Reed Smoot: An Apostle in Politics*. Salt Lake City: Utah State University Press.

Morison, Elting Elmore. 1960. *Turmoil and Tradition: A Study of the Life and Times of Henry L. Stimson*. Boston: Houghton Mifflin.

Nash, Ogden. 1931. *Hard Lines*. New York: Simon & Schuster.

Nevins, Allan. 1950. *The United States in a Chaotic World*. New Haven: Yale University Press.

Porter, Kirk H., and Donald B. Johnson. 1956. *National Party Platforms: 1840–1956*. Urbana: University of Illinois Press.

Reagan, Ronald. 1984. *Public Papers of the President of the United States, 1983*. Washington, DC: Government Printing Office.

———. 1988. *Public Papers of the President of the United States, 1985*. Washington, DC: Government Printing Office.

Richardson, Gary, and William Troost. 2009. "Monetary Intervention Mitigated Banking Panics During the Great Depression." *Journal of Political Economy* 117, 1031–74.

Rogers, Will. 1978. *Will Rogers' Daily Telegrams. Vol. 2: The Hoover Years, 1929–31*, edited by James M. Smallwood and Steven K. Gragert. Stillwater: Oklahoma State University Press.

Romer, Christina D. 1990. "The Great Crash and the Onset of the Great Depression." *Quarterly Journal of Economics* 105, 597–624.

———. 1992. "What Ended the Great Depression?" *Journal of Economic History* 52, 757–84.

———. 1993. "The Nation in Depression." *Journal of Economic Perspectives* 7, 19–40.

Salter, Sir Arthur. 1932. *Recovery: The Second Effort.* London: G. Bell & Sons.

———. 1961. *Memoirs of a Public Servant.* London: Faber.

Schattschneider, E. E. 1935. *Politics, Pressure, and the Tariff.* New York: Prentice Hall.

Schnietz, Karen. 2000. "The Institutional Foundations of U.S. Trade Policy: Revisiting Explanations for the 1934 Reciprocal Trade Agreements Act." *Journal of Policy History* 12, 417–44.

Schwartz, Anna J. 1981. "Understanding 1929–1933." In *The Great Depression Revisited*, edited by Karl Brunner. Boston: Martinus Nijhoff.

Scroggs, William O. 1930. "Revolt against the Tariff." *North American Review* 230, 18–24.

Sherman, John. 1895. *Recollections of Forty Years in the House, Senate, and Cabinet.* Chicago: Werner Co.

Slichter, Sumner H. 1932. "Is the Tariff a Cause of the Depression?" *Current History* 35, 519–24.

Smith, Howard R., and John F. Hart. 1955. "The American Tariff Map." *Geographical Review* 45, 327–46.

Smith, Richard Norton. 1984. *An Uncommon Man: the Triumph of Herbert Hoover.* New York: Simon & Schuster.

Smoot, Reed. 1931. "Our Tariff and the Depression." *Current History* 35, 173–81.

Snyder, J. Richard. 1973. "Hoover and the Hawley-Smoot Tariff: A View of Executive Leadership." *Annals of Iowa* 41, 1173–89.

Steel, Ronald. 1980. *Walter Lippmann and the American Century.* Boston: Little, Brown.

Stein, Ben. 2007. "The Smoot-Hawley Act Is More than a Laugh Line." *New York Times*, May 10.

Sumner, Scott. 1992. "The Role of the International Gold Standard in Commodity Price Deflation: Evidence from the 1929 Stock Market Crash." *Explorations in Economic History* 29, 290–317.

Sundquist, James L. 1983. *Dynamics of the Party System: Alignment and Realignment of Political Parties in the United States.* Washington, DC: Brookings Institution.

Taft, Robert A. 1997–2006. *The Papers of Robert A. Taft,* edited by Clarence E. Wunderlin, Jr. 4 vols. Kent, OH: Kent State University Press.

Taussig, Frank W. 1920. "Cost of Production and the Tariff." In *Free Trade, the Tariff, and Reciprocity.* New York: Macmillan.

——. 1929. "The Tariff Bill and Our Friends Abroad." *Foreign Affairs* 8, 1–12.

——. 1930. "The Tariff Act of 1930." *Quarterly Journal of Economics* 45, 1–21.

Temin, Peter. 1989. *Lessons from the Great Depression.* Cambridge: MIT Press.

Temin, Peter, and Barrie Wigmore. 1990. "End to One Big Deflation." *Explorations in Economic History* 27, 483–502.

Truman, Harry S. 1963. *Public Papers of the President of the United States, 1947.* Washington, DC: Government Printing Office.

U.S. Department of Commerce. 1976. *Historical Statistics of the United States: Bicentennial Edition.* Washington, DC: Government Printing Office.

U.S. Tariff Commission. 1930. "Comparison of Rates of Duty in Pending Tariff Bill of 1929." Senate Document No. 119. 71st Congress, 2d Session. Washington, DC: Government Printing Office.

——. 1931. "Imports into the United States from Principal Countries." Washington, DC: Government Printing Office.

Wanniski, Jude. 1978. *The Way the World Works.* New York: Basic Books.

White, Eugene N. 1984. "A Reinterpretation of the Banking Crisis of 1930." *Journal of Economic History* 44, 119–38.

——. 1990a. "The Stock Market Boom and Crash of 1929 Revisited." *Journal of Economic Perspectives* 4, 67–83.

——. 1990b. "When the Ticker Ran Late: The Stock Market Boom and Crash of 1929." In *Crises and Panics: The Lessons of History,* edited by Eugene N. White. Homewood: Dow Jones– Irwin.

Wicker, Elmus. 1996. *Banking Panics of the Great Depression.* New York: Cambridge University Press.

Index

Note: Page numbers in *italics* indicate illustrations; those with a *t* indicate tables.